A Child's Life 90 Years Ago

Recollections of Florence and Earle Ahlquist
1923–1946, Scarborough, Maine

A Child's Life
90 Years Ago

Recollections of Florence and Earle Ahlquist
1923–1946, Scarborough, Maine

COMPILED AND WRITTEN BY
EARLENE AHLQUIST CHADBOURNE

CUSTOM COMMUNICATIONS
PUBLISHER
Saco, Maine

A Child's Life 90 Years Ago: Recollections of Florence and Earle Ahlquist, 1923-1946, Scarborough, ME
Copyright © 2019 by Earlene Ahlquist Chadbourne. All rights reserved.

Published by:
Custom Communications, Inc.
7 Pilgrim Lane, Saco ME 04072
www.desktoppub.com

Earlene Ahlquist Chadbourne
50 Stockholm Drive, Cumberland, ME 04021

Library of Congress Preassigned Control Number: 2019930018
ISBN: 1-892168-23-5
ISBN-13: 978-1-892168-23-8

Edited by Susan Dudley Gold
Layout, typography, and setup: Custom Communications, Inc.

Cover: Family photo
Photography: All photographs provided by family members except the following:
p. 64, Photograph from the Collections of Haystack Historical Society. Used with permission from the Maine Historical Society.; p. 72, Photograph from the Collections of Maine Historical Society. Used with permission from the Maine Historical Society; p. 141, U.S. National Archives; p. 146, Sagredo/Commons:Wikimedia; p. 148, Center for Public Domain/W. Wolny/Commons: Wikimedia; p. 150, Photo 26-G-4140, U.S. Department of Transportation, U.S. Coast Guard, Office of Public and International Affairs/Commons: Wikimedia.

1 3 5 6 4 2

Contents

Preface

I am the daughter of Earle N. Ahlquist and the niece of Florence Ahlquist Link, who were siblings. They were two years apart in age, the eldest children of Rudolph and Marjorie (Chadbourn) Ahlquist. In the last years of their long lives, they lived in two separate nursing homes. Though they each tried to be cheerful adaptors to their new surroundings, I knew they needed a new focus. Having heard them speak often of growing up during the Depression in rural Scarborough, Maine, I proposed to them a series of interviews so that I could write their stories for their great-grandchildren. They both jumped at the chance to share their early childhood recollections. Knowing that today's world is quite different from that of their growing up years, they adopted this new mission in life. They believed that preserving their family history was just as valuable as the roles they had filled as heads of their families, and it was unique to them—no one else could tell their story.

Armed with a rough draft, timeline, photos, recipes (that I collected from family), and a notebook, I visited each of them regularly. Aunt Flonnie was particularly good at recalling in-house details; Dad provided clear descriptions of the outdoor and barn work. Dad's stories, in particular, were rich with details. I added to my research by consulting Scarborough town records and the archives at the Maine Historical Society. I read the accounts myself, then read them to Flonnie and Dad to check for accuracy, and made corrections according to their suggestions. The banter between sister and brother, conveyed by me as the go-between, was both fun and helpful. We proceeded systematically—and the more I read them their recollections, the more their memories revealed. They were not the only ones enthusiastic about the project; their nursing home neighbors became eager to hear the next chapters as well.

The two of them related not only the big events of their youth—growing up in the Depression and serving in WWII—they also remembered when electricity first came to their 1750 farmhouse, when their road was first paved, and how they had to negotiate travel in a Ford Model T or horse and wagon. They remembered the icy fear that struck their hearts when their mother had to be hospitalized and their resolve to keep their fears to themselves when they determined to step up and keep the farm running so their father could take on outside work to help pay the medical bills. They remembered being aware of growing conflict in Europe as the war approached America and anxiety over the fate of cousins who lived in Norway. They recalled the family's innovative approach—despite those tensions—to the economic challenges posed by the Depression, and they recalled the silly ways of childhood and their gratefulness for the constant presence of family and friends.

They remembered their amazing parents, who set the standard for facing the world with humor, honesty, and integrity, and their mother's remarkable memory as she shared poems and stories from her childhood—poems that years later would be given to the University of Maine folk-telling inventory, then later as part of the Library of Congress Archives. These poems and stories became a central feature of their bedtime ritual throughout their early lives.

They remembered words and lessons of their parents that had guided them throughout their lives, even into old age. They were nurtured by the emotional security found in their parent's love, trust, and belief in them. Over and over, I could see how Proverbs 22:6—"Train up a child in the way he should go, and when he is old, he will not depart from it" —had proven true.

When stories refer to Dad—it is their father, Rudolph E. Ahlquist; Mama is their mother, Marjorie Chadbourn Ahlquist; Ma is their grandmother, Marta Karine Ahlquist; Pa is their grandfather, August C. Ahlquist. The graph at the front of the book lists close family they interacted with growing up.

Enjoy!

—Earlene Ahlquist Chadbourne

Fall 2018

CHAPTER 1
Recollections of Life on Oak Knoll Farm

Located on the knoll of a hill on Beech Ridge Road in Scarborough, Maine, Oak Knoll Farm was built in the 1700s. John Meserve, one of the first town leaders of Scarborough, originally lived in the farmhouse, a substantial building with a large center chimney to accommodate several fireplaces and a hiding place from Indians. An offset addition, attached to the original building, became the kitchen and a connecting ell, making the farmhouse quite large. A sixteen-foot porch rimmed the south side of the house.

This is the farm as it looked when Rudolph and Marjorie Ahlquist gazed longingly at it and yearned to make it their own. Newly married—the wedding was on July 10, 1923—the young couple believed the farmhouse would soon come on the market because the owner, Alfred Goudy, was elderly and in poor health. When Mr. Goudy died, they approached the estate and arranged to buy the farm. The purchase was completed on November 26, 1923, a date Marjorie considered to be propitious, because it marked the wedding anniversary of her loving grandparents, who had raised her. By then, her parents and grandparents had died, and her brothers had joined the Coast Guard. She was building a new home with her beloved husband, and that special date gave her a sense of their blessing. She applied her inheritance to the purchase price of the farm. Once the papers were filed at the Registry of Deeds on Nov. 27, 1923, the Ahlquist family began moving the newlyweds into their new-old farm.

This was the farm, situated on 60 acres of land with several outbuildings, that would become a useful and productive part of the community again. No longer would the good soil lay fallow. And the house would

Elton and Georgie (Ahlquist) Getchell and Marjorie (Chadbourn) and Rudolph E. Ahlquist wedding day—July 10, 1923

became a home echoing the voices of lively children. Rudolph and Marjorie faced the world with hope.

It was here where Florence Lucretia Ahlquist was born in June 1924. She was the first child born in this old house in 100 years. Her grandmother, Marta Karine Ahlquist, helped deliver her into the world. Dr. Wentworth registered her birth with the town. He registered her birth as June 16—she was actually born at 3 a.m. on June 17—so the family always celebrated two birthdays, one on each day. Marjorie and Marta and Rudolph's sisters, Georgie, Harriette, Albertine, and Ruth, had been making baby clothes for months before the birth to welcome Florence into the family. There was great celebration!

Twenty-three months later Florence was joined by her brother, Earle Norris Ahlquist, born on the first official Mother's Day, on May 9, 1926.

Three other children followed to fill out the family. After Earle's arrival, Marjorie gave birth to a set of twins, who died. Joy followed sadness when Edward August Ahlquist was born in August 1929, followed by Leroy Arnold Ahlquist, born in April 1931. Then, in the middle of a fierce snowstorm, Pauline Ruth Jayne Ahlquist was born in January 1935.

This is the story of the joys and struggles of these children growing up surrounded by a loving family. This is the story of Florence whose love for learning and family brought forth goodness from the children she nurtured. This is the story of Earle, who became a kind and good man from a loving boy with adventure on his mind. These stories are written for the great-grandchildren in hopes they will come to understand and appreciate the roots of their heritage.

Proverbs 20:7
The godly walk with integrity, blessed are their children who follow them.

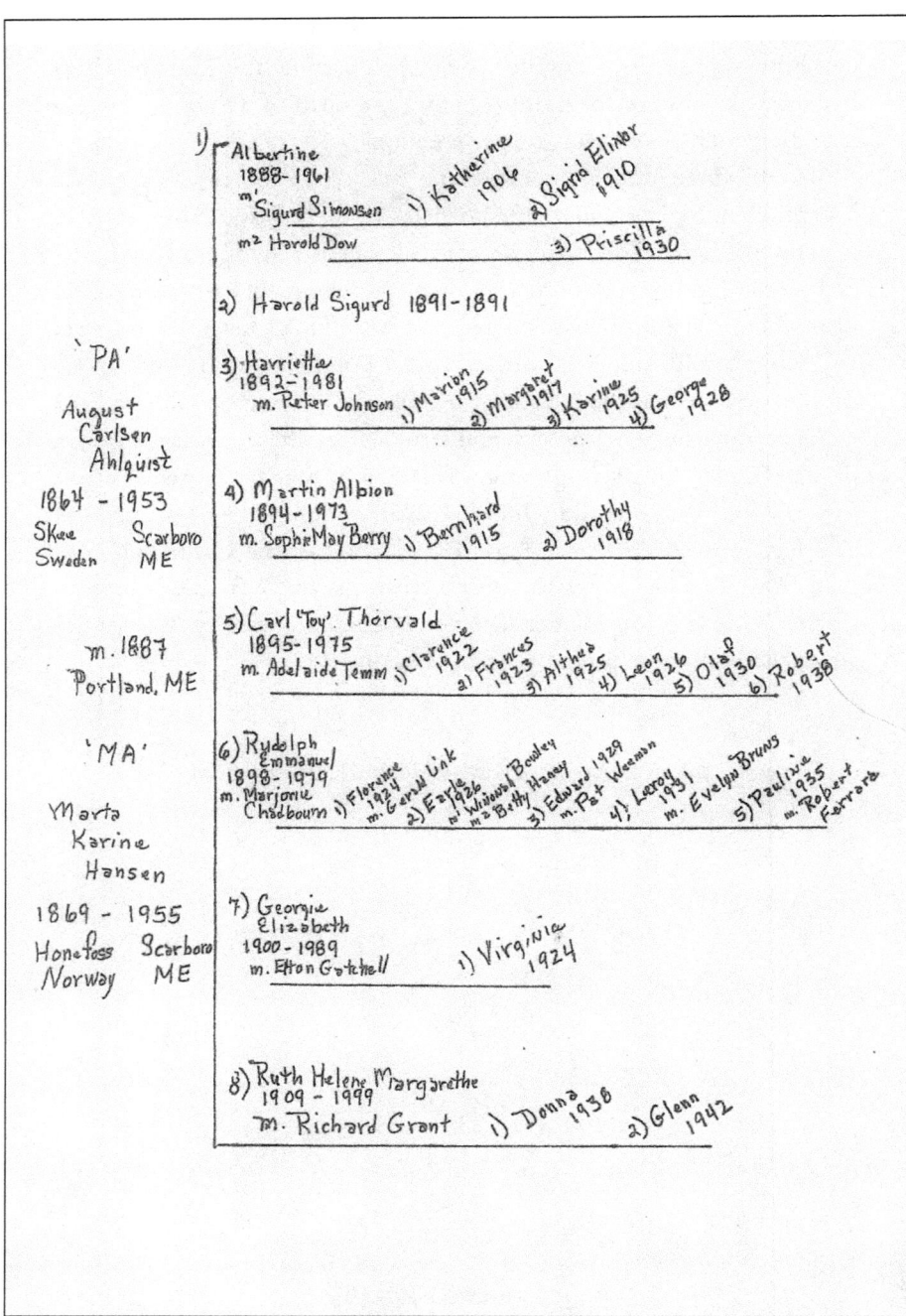

'PA'

August
Carlsen
Ahlquist

1864 - 1953
Skiæ   Scarboro
Sweden   ME

m. 1887
Portland, ME

'MA'

Marta
Karine
Hansen

1869 - 1955
Honefoss   Scarboro
Norway   ME

1) Albertine
1888 - 1961
m¹ Sigurd Simonsen   1) Katherine 1906   2) Sigrid Elinor 1910
m² Harold Dow   3) Priscilla 1930

2) Harold Sigurd 1891 - 1891

3) Harriette
1892 - 1981
m. Peter Johnson   1) Marion 1915   2) Margaret 1917   3) Karine 1925   4) George 1928

4) Martin Albion
1894 - 1973
m. Sophie May Berry   1) Bernhard 1915   2) Dorothy 1918

5) Carl 'Toy' Thorvald
1895 - 1975
m. Adelaide Temm   1) Clarence 1922   2) Frances 1923   3) Althea 1925   4) Leon 1926   5) Olaf 1930   6) Robert 1938

6) Rudolph
Emmanuel
1898 - 1979
m. Marjorie
Chadbourn   1) Florence 1924   2) Eagle 1926   3) Edward 1929   4) Leroy 1931   5) Pauline 1935
m. Gerald Link   m¹ Wideawa Bowley   m. Pat Weeman   m. Evelyn Bruns   m. Robert Ferrara
                 m² Betty Haney

7) Georgie
Elizabeth
1900 - 1989
m. Elton Gatchell   1) Virginia 1924

8) Ruth Helene Margarethe
1909 - 1999
m. Richard Grant   1) Donna 1938   2) Glenn 1942

CHAPTER 2
Ma

Ma was Dad's mother. Her actual name was Marta Karine Haagensdatter. When she came to America at age seventeen, her name was shortened to Hansen. Ma was born on February 26, 1869, the third child of eleven in Honefoss, Norway. She was often called Kari. She was sturdy, bright, and resourceful, and to her grandchildren, she always seemed cheerfully busy. She and August married on November 5, 1887, each having been in America about a year.

Several of Ma's relatives, including a sister and brother, had already immigrated to Maine, giving her the courage to come alone at age sixteen. She arranged to meet her sister Thea and brother Andreas in Portland, Maine, where a few aunts and uncles had already settled. They had traveled in groups, but Ma set out all alone. She boarded the ship *Rollo* in Norway. Traveling steerage, she had one carrying case and wore all seven of her petticoats to conserve space. She spoke only Norwegian and had two silver American dollars and Thea's address in Portland.

The ship stopped first in Scotland to take on more passengers, then sailed on to Montreal, Canada, where Ma had to take a train to Portland. It took her six weeks to complete the trip, during which she celebrated her seventeenth birthday. She confided to grandson Earle years later that though the journey was at times perilous, confusing, and difficult, she never thought it was a mistake and was determined to keep her own counsel with herself and her God, ever sure that she was on the right path and it would be honored. A practical girl, she packed cheese, crackers, dried fruit, and nuts. Each day she measured out her daily provisions of food carefully. She had determined before setting out that she would have to tend to her own health on the journey.

13

Marta Karine Hansen and August Ahlquist on their wedding day, Nov. 5, 1887.

"What was the hardest part of the voyage?" Earle once asked her.

Looking clearly at her grandson, Ma said, "After stopping at Scotland lots of passengers boarded, all crowded into steerage. I learned to get along with most even though I did not speak their tongue. But there was a young couple with a newborn baby. The parents were foolish and did not know how to care for the babe. It cried a lot. I felt so bad for the baby and the mother. One night it cried almost all night, then suddenly it stopped, I drifted back to sleep. When I awoke, the baby was missing. I think they threw it overboard. I was almost sick to my stomach when I realized what had happened."

Earle gulped and thought about it for a moment. He could see the tears in her eyes.

"Don't tell this to others, Earle," she told him. "They don't need to know. This is why I work so hard to care for children. It's not that parents don't love their children. It is just that so many of them are simply stupid!"

Later, as they gathered eggs or headed to the barn to milk cows, Ma told Earle that as a child in Norway she had to herd goats in the hill country. It was challenging to keep them safe from the elements and wild animals. She became skilled in her care of animals. She proved to be resourceful and focused on strength and safety. Some of the farmers she worked for were not very kind, though, and that made things difficult.

She added to her skills by helping her mother with midwife tasks, knowing these skills would be helpful in the future. Though she loved her family and her beautiful Norway, she also knew there was little future there for her because it was a small country with many people. When older relatives wrote about their new home in America, the young Kari began to dream of life in America. She spoke to her parents about her wish, and they saved and planned to make that possible.

Before the journey, Andreas sent her detailed descriptions of where to go when she landed in Canada, how to get to the train station, and how to spot the train that would take her to Portland. He also included some coins to help with her expenses. He knew his little sister would use her common sense.

It was a great relief when the ship arrived in Canada. Kari was filled with optimism. All this she recounted to Earle as he brought her home from his house. Suddenly she asked him to detour to a neighbor's home. She wanted to check on sickly children. She knew they were battling what might turn into pneumonia. Earle waited in the wagon and watched as his grandmother entered the house.

After comforting the neighbor, Mrs. Smith, and offering advice on how to care for the children, she said, "These children need fresh oranges."

"I don't know if that can be done," Mrs. Smith replied as she fearfully looked to where her husband was in the barn.

August & Marta Karine Ahlquist c. 1940

Knowing the family was poor and that Mr. Smith had a reputation for putting things off, Ma patted Mrs. Smith's hands and said, "I will take care of it."

With sureness of step, Ma strode through the open barn door and addressed the man: "Mr. Smith, the children need oranges."

"By and by, Mrs. Ahlquist," he replied.

Deftly grasping a nearby pitchfork and quickly pointing it in his direction, Ma replied, "Now, Mr. Smith. Now!"

"Yes, Mrs. Ahlquist," the startled man responded, then quickly mounted his horse and headed out of the barn, presumably to the store to fetch the required oranges.

Only then, did Ma get back in the wagon so Earle could continue driving her home. Ma did not want any children to suffer on her watch, espcially when common sense measures could be taken to prevent it. This dedication earned Ma the respect of nearby physicians like Dr. Wentworth and Dr. Stickney. When patients in the rural area needed attention, these doctors often contacted Ma to step in and help them care for those in need. Her skill was well-recognized not only in the family but throughout the community. She called on that skill in the fall of 1925 when two granddaughters, Althea and Karine, were born within a short time of each other. Ma was busy that day. It was a good thing both young mothers took the precaution of moving temporarily to the farmhouse before the births.

Ma's ability to address a problem wasn't limited to illnesses. When Earle raised a young ox and wanted to enter it in a 4-H competition, he faced an awkward challenge to which Ma devised a surprising solution.

Though Earle had trained the young ox well, its horns did not match; one was malformed and somewhat twisted. He feared the mismatched horns would count against his ox in the competition.

Ma said, "Earle , we can fix this. Bring in wood for a hot fire."

Obediently, he did. She put her waiting bread dough in the oven to bake. As soon as the bread was done, Ma told Earle to hold the head of the young ox firmly. Quickly Ma thrust the hot bread onto the malformed horn. She kept it there for a few minutes while Earle steadied the animal by speaking to it soothingly. When Ma removed the bread, she firmly reshaped the horn to match the other.

Earle and his ox won first place!

"Pa" August Carlson Ahlquist about 1935

CHAPTER 3
Pa

Pa (August Ahlquist) thought it most important to teach his ten grandsons—born from 1915 to 1942—how to be responsible and make their way in the world with honesty, respectful behavior, and decency. Pa was born in 1864 in Skee, Sweden, close to the Norwegian border. Norway and Sweden were a combined country at that time.

In Sweden, Pa's childhood home, where it is dark as night even during the daytime during the winter months, children learned how to find their location by looking to the stars and using them as "landmarks." The stars remained fixed and shown brightly at night. Constellations took on shapes of wild animals, which helped children to identify them: the Big Dipper, the Little Dipper, the North Star, Leo the Lion, the Ram, the Bear, the Horse and Rider, and the Arrow—all names the boys could remember. Though they shifted during the change of seasons the star formations remained fixed relative to each other—rather like a map.

Using the stars to navigate became an even more vital skill once August became a seven-year-old cabin boy on his grandfather's ship in 1871. He left Fredrickstad, Norway, and sailed all around the world, learning many languages and skills along the way. He advanced through several stages of nautical training and passed a series of certifications. But when he came to America and met Marta Karine, he decided it was time to trade his sailing life for a more stable occupation. Pa's brother, Anton Carlson, got him a job as a patent-maker at the Berlin, New Hampshire, mills. After working all week, he boarded the train to Portland on weekends to visit Marta Karine.

By the time the first grandsons came along, Pa had retired from his work as captain of E. B. Winslow's scow in Casco Bay. Even so, he was still responsive as a grandfather when it came to teaching the young Ahlquists. Though Pa was never one to talk much about himself, the boys occasionally were able to draw stories out of him that shed light on his life when he was a younger man. He taught his grandsons how to read the stars and locate where they were in relationship to the stars. Unbeknownst to them at the time, that skill would someday become vital, when they were in the woods at night or on the ocean. If the grandsons ever got lost, they had the skills to find their way.

Cousin George and Earle were at Ma and Pa's one day. They had finished helping saw and split logs and stack them and were asking Pa some questions. Pa told them the most important man in his young life had been his grandfather, the ship captain, because his father had disappeared when he was very young. Aunt Ruth had told them earlier that Pa's father had come to America to fight for the North in the Civil War, about the same time Pa was born in Sweden. Pa's father had come so that he could gain a tract of land in America—a payment for fighting. Pa's father never returned to Sweden. But Pa did know his grandfather, who taught him how to navigate in the ocean, how to become an engineer, and how to get along in many different countries.

During the visit, Pa showed the boys several military ribbons and medals that had been awarded to family members. The blue and yellow ribbons with fancy medals attached to them thrilled the boys. They weren't allowed to play with them. Pa carefully put them back into his cigar box and put them away as he took out his pipe and tapped loose tobacco into it, lit a match, and took a smoke.

Years later, youngest grandson Glenn recalled how Pa, though blind by then, took a scythe and used it to steady his steps he walked out to the backyard of the farm to the steep gully. Swinging the scythe with measured rhythm, pausing to step forward while using the scythe to gauge his steps, he felled the hay for the farm and never fell down the steep bank. By the time he finished, the bank was shorn clean. Glenn raked up the cut hay for the animals.

About that same time, after Earle had returned from the service, he drove Pa to Westbrook for a haircut. They had to wait their turn as Red the Barber did his work. Several men were already in line and chatting in a language Earle did not understand. Pa started to laugh and joined in the conversation with the chatting men. Earle was surprised. Upon returning home, Earle asked Pa how he came to understand those men who spoke a different language. Pa eventually admitted to Earle that he could speak, read, and write seven different languages, a skill he had learned while traveling around the world as a young seaman.

Pa told Earle that his father had come to America, been promised land if he fought in the Civil War; but then drowned in the Mississippi River. As his father's son, Pa had received a notice that he could claim the land in Minnesota, but Ma had been adamant that she would not travel farther west., so they never went. Ma always missed Norway and sometimes liked to go to the Atlantic Ocean, where she could look east and know that Norway was out there.

Pa valued the right to vote highly and believed everyone who was eligible should cast a ballot. Voting was a privilege that was denied to him in Sweden, which at that time had certain restrictions on who could vote. Pa also treasured the right to own your own home, work your own land, and send your children to school in America.

The radio and newspapers kept him up to date on news and sports. He loved following baseball games on the radio. Until he became blind, he always read the Swedish, Norwegian, and American newspapers daily.

When two of his three sons became a bit wild in their teenage years, Pa promptly enlisted them in the Coast Guard to help them gain discipline. He did not require that of Rudolph, who responded with more self-discipline, though ultimately all three sons served in World War I.

At Christmastime, when the extended Ahlquist family gathered, the men cleared the living room of furniture to provide dancing space. Rudolph played the fiddle, Georgie played the concertina, Marjorie played the piano, and Ma and Pa led the dancing around the Christmas tree. Earle and Florence remembered being amazed at how young their grandparents seemed as they twirled and stepped a unique style of dancing with a special half-step twist from the old country. It was fun to watch. Pa never returned to Sweden or Norway. He never wanted to. He was always proud to call himself an American.

Aerial view of Oak Knoll Farm about 1955.

CHAPTER 4
Oak Knoll Farm—Early Years

Earle and Flonnie seemed destined to be overachievers. They were happy, healthy, blue-eyed blondes who settled into the farm household, both intent on becoming helpers as they followed their parents around and copied them as they worked the farm.

Flonnie started helping Mama early on, carefully cleaning the lanterns nightly and setting the table, mending clothes, or feeding the chickens and gathering eggs.

Earle walked at seven months and hardly stopped as soon as he could totter along. He followed Dad everywhere he went, whether bringing wood in for the fireplaces and cook stove or tending the cows in the barn. Earle often accompanied Dad as he visited and worked with the other men in the area. Young Earle became Rudolph's shadow as they did men's work about the farm. Rudolph enjoyed the companionship of his son and often asked his opinion, encouraging Earle's ability to consider a situation. Both Rudolph and Marjorie thought it important to teach their children to think things through, a skill they practiced during lively discussions at the dinner table.

Work on the farm was done in an orderly fashion. The care of animals and farm equipment followed a set schedule. Every Monday the family lugged water in pails from the nearby spring. They all marched to the spring with pails and dipped them in the cool water. Back they marched to the house, where they filled a big double boiler, attached to the Dutch oven in the kitchen, where the Queen Atlantic wood stove was set up. Monday was always washing day; they used hot water to clean the clothes by hand.

The summer kitchen connected the kitchen to the outer tool shed. It

Mama with turkey hens—about 1925

served as an important work and storage room. A big round metal wash tub stored on a wall hook served many purposes. Saturday night it was used for family baths, and on Monday morning it became the wash tub for laundry.

The heated water was put in the tub, and soiled clothes were submerged into the sudsy water as Mama added soap and Flonnie stirred with a wooden paddle to produce bubbles. Carefully Mama scrubbed the clothes and wrung them out with her hands, then deposited them into another tub with cooler water. Sometimes Earle helped, but mostly Flonnie did this. After clothes were removed from the second tub and wrung out a second time, Mama took them to the back of the house, where Dad had strung a rope to hang the clean clothes to dry in the sun and wind. On cold or rainy days the clothes dried on wooden racks set up in the summer kitchen.

Regardless of what Mama cooked for the main meal at supper time, the family often had Washing Cake (her grandmother's recipe) for dessert. It was a plain cake that had a nutmeg or lemon or chocolate sauce on it instead of frosting. Mama had been raised by her grandmother after her own mother died.

Washing Cake

Mix together ¼ pound of melted butter with ⅔ cup sugar and 1 large egg. In a separate bowl, mix with a clean fork: 2-2 ½ cups flour with 1 teaspoon cream of tartar and ½ teaspoon baking soda. Pour ⅔ cup sweet milk and 1 teaspoon vanilla into a measuring cup. Then add everything together, stirring thoroughly. Grease and flour a 6"x10" pan and pour the batter into it. Bring the oven heat up to about 350 degrees and bake this cake for about 25 minutes. As it is baking make the hot sweet sauce to go over it.

Lemon Sauce:

Mix with a fork: 1 cup sugar and 2 tablespoons cornstarch. Mix thoroughly. Add 2 cups of boiling water and cook until it appears clear. Add 2 Tablespoons butter, 2 tablespoons lemon juice and a dash of nutmeg. Serve warm over cake that has been cut and put in saucers or small bowls. Yummy!

While Flonnie was learning how to wash clothes and cook, four-year-old Earle learned to milk cows. The most gentle cow was named Blossom, so she became Earle's special cow.

Blossom was a Guernsey cow with big gentle brown eyes, and the brown-black hair on her right foreleg looked like the letters U and S. Earle arose early in the morning with Dad and marched to the barn where the cows lived. Dad hung the lantern up so they could see. They spoke gently and reassuringly to the cows. First they fed the cows with hay, grain, and fresh water. This settled the cows down so they relaxed to be milked. Dad pulled up a three-legged stool and showed Earle how to sit still near the full udders of Blossom. Firmly but gently grasping the udder with a full hand, Earle first pressed upward with his fist against the udder to signal that milking time had begun. He learned to squeeze each teat gently, aiming the milk so it would fall into the pail below. Then he lightly patted the udder, as if to thank Blossom for giving her milk. When Earle was five years old, he milked two cows a day.

Several cats lived in the barn to keep mice away and were company for the cows. They often rubbed up next to Earle as he milked. Carefully copying his father's actions, Earle usually turned Blossom's teat just a bit and squirted warm milk into a nearby bowl for the cats to enjoy before he filled the milk pail. Blossom gave good rich milk. Earle knew that this would be used for the family to cook with, drink, make butter, and in the summer, ice cream! So taking care of Blossom and the other cows became an important job for him. Over the years more cows were added, so that twelve cows eventually comprised the herd. All of them had names, all gave sweet milk, but Blossom remained Earle's favorite.

CHAPTER 5
The Rooster—A Short But Eventful Life!

Four-year-old Earle was off with Dad. They were visiting Sam Scott at his farm on the Holmes Road. Sam was a sawyer with a small farm. Earle always liked travelling with Dad, visiting interesting men, doing men's work.

As the men talked, Earle became interested in Sam's handsome flock of chickens. They were particularly striking, with a few roosters that were very handsome—unusual to Earle's way of thinking because this flock sported very colorful feathers. This prompted Earle to say, "I'd like to have that beautiful rooster, Mr. Scott."

Focusing his attention on the tow-headed boy, Sam replied, "Well, if you give me ten cents, you can have that rooster. Now I want ten pennies, not a dime, and not two nickels." Probably thinking the child would never be able to do that, Sam went back to his conversation with Rudolph. But Earle went home with a mission.

Within a week, Earle and his father again went to see Sam Scott. Earle reached into his pocket and counted out ten pennies. Impressed, Sam—a man of his word—picked up the handsome rooster and deposited it into Earle's outstretched arms. Earle was sure this would be a handsome addition to his mother's flock. Perhaps he had overheard that the handsome Ancona chickens would be an upgrade to American flocks.

Unfortunately for Earle, that rooster had a particularly mean disposition and did not hesitate to demonstrate it. When Earle tried to pick him up, he flew up and pecked at Earle's head—very painfully. Earle dropped him immediately and tried to stay away from the rooster.

Within a few months this Ancona addition to the flock quietly disappeared, and peace was restored. The family enjoyed chicken and dumplings that evening! Oh, so good! No one seemed to miss Ancona. It was a learning experience for Earle.

Chicken and Dumplings

Cut chicken for stewing. Place in kettle with enough cool water to cover and simmer gently for an hour. Season with 1 teaspoon salt, 2 whole cloves, a sprig of parsley, ¼ teaspoon pepper and a few leaves of celery. The seasonings can be put in a cheesecloth bag and removed later. Simmer until chicken is tender but not falling apart.

In the meantime make dumpling batter. Sift together 1 cup flour, 2 teaspoons baking powder, and ¼ teaspoon salt. Then mix in 1 large beaten egg with ⅓ to ½ cup of milk. Stir only until mixed.

Bring the chicken to a boil and drop the dumplings by spoonfuls over the boiling mixture. Cover and steam 15 minutes before removing the lid.

CHAPTER 6
School Days

Beech Ridge School was located about a mile from Oak Knoll farm. Neighborhood children walked to school. The children walked together to the corner of Holmes Road, where the Sweet Shop was located, then turned right. Beech Ridge School was located on the left hand side of the road. It was a two-room wooden schoolhouse that served grades one through eight, with one teacher who taught all the children.

Florence began school in 1929 a few weeks after Edward was born. She was a quick student and enjoyed school. Mama had introduced her to the Westbrook library, where she had borrowed books for a few years. Flonnie could read before she entered first grade and thoroughly enjoyed the learning opportunities she found at school. Cousin Frances Ahlquist was a year ahead of her in school. Twenty to thirty students attended the little school during that time.

New students visited the school the day before they were scheduled to start. So in early September 1931, Earle walked to school with sister Florence. It was set to be a half day of school for the visitors, with the new students dismissed to go home at the noon break.

When Florence and Earle entered the white wooden schoolhouse, they faced a rather large room with many school desks all facing the teacher's desk, which was in the middle of the front room. A blackboard covered one whole wall, extending from the ceiling to three feet from the floor. Neatly scripted letters and numbers ran across the top of the blackboard. A large, round wood stove stood to the right of the big room. The two side walls each had two sets of windows to view the outside. Beyond the schoolroom was a small but very useful room. It

Florence and Earle, first day of school, 1931.

held the kitchen, a woodshed, and a hall with two doors that led to the outhouses—one served the boys and the other was for the girls. Each outhouse held a bench with holes over which the boy—or girl—sat to take care of necessary bathroom needs. There was no running water.

A tall, sturdy, smiling woman greeted them. She introduced herself as Miss Haskell, their teacher.

Class opened at 8:30 A.M with an outdoor recess break about 10 A.M for half an hour and lunch break at noon. School closed at 3 P.M.

All students rose for the morning exercises, faced the American flag in the corner of the room, placed their right hands over their hearts, and recited in unison the Pledge of Allegiance to the Flag. This was followed by bowing their heads and together saying The Lord's Prayer and singing a song. During milder weather, the flag flew outside at the flagpole.

Students then started on their assignments, which were posted on the blackboard. Either mid-morning or sometimes mid-afternoon, Miss

Haskell read a chapter from one of the classic books like *Treasure Island*, *Heidi*, *Black Beauty*, or others.

When recess break arrived, the children went outside to play. The girls usually skipped rope or played games together, while the boys played on the other side of the playground. That first day Earle noticed the larger boys playing roughly with the much younger, smaller boys. Earle stayed back and watched carefully.

Soon it was time for the new students to head back to their homes after receiving their initiation to public school. Earle had things to think about.

The next morning Earle awoke with a plan in hand. After Mama packed their lunch pails with enough food to share with other students, Florence and Earle—accompanied by Earle's dog, Chub—headed off to school.

Miss Haskell was waiting for the children as they arrived at school. Seeing Chub standing obediently next to Earle, she kindly remarked, "Young man, you cannot bring your dog to the schoolroom." Looking confidently at Miss Haskell, Earle replied, "If my dog can't come to school, I won't come either." Surprised, Miss Haskell nodded, allowing Chub in the building, thinking perhaps this would be the only day. Chub proceeded into the room and calmly lay next to Earle's desk the entire day, arising only when Earle did. When recess came, the bigger boys never bothered the younger boys, and everyone had fun. Lunch was the same. At the end of the day, they all walked home.

The entire year progressed much the same way, with Chub accompanying Earle to school every day. At the end of the year Miss Haskell told Earle that Chub's attendance at school had been a very good thing. Chub's presence had served to dissuade the bigger boys from bullying the young ones.

The following year the older boys all joined the Conservation Corps and no longer attended public school.

Florence and Earle and their dog, Chub.

CHAPTER 7
Chub

Chub was Earle's very special dog. Animals filled specific roles on Oak Knoll Farm, primarily related to the manner in which they contributed to the industry of the farm. Horses were used for plowing and transportation, cows provided milk and food. Rabbits contributed angora fur. Cats kept rodents under control. Chicken and geese furnished eggs and food. Pigs were raised for food. Dogs herded and controlled the other animals.

Chub, however, was special. Initially, he was the only animal allowed in the house. He slept next to Earle's bed and accompanied him wherever he could.

Chub was born on the farm. His mother, named Judy, was a "laughing collie," because she always looked like she was smiling. She was the primary herder for the cows and horses. Chub's father was a shepherd named Pal. He protected the herds and helped herd the cows and horses into the barn. Chub was a big dog and devoted to Earle. Chub was about a year old when he started school with Earle, and he remained a devoted companion, always taking clues from Earle and sensing what needed to be done around the farm and doing it.

In 1944 Chub and Earle faced a challenge—very akin to the challenges Earle and his human family faced—when Earle enlisted in the Marine Corps to fight in World War II and faced real danger. Chub felt Earle's absence intensely. Human loved ones, of course, missed Earle, too, and worried when communication was spotty, which it usually was. But Chub got no comfort from the limited communications from Earle, and the dog's frustration, sadness, and confusion were hard to remedy.

The family gathered together to host a going away gathering in Earle's honor before he left for the war. It was an unspoken rule that everyone would be positive, cheerful, and hopeful that the war would end soon. Earle managed his emotions well until Chub put both forepaws on his master's shoulders and kissed his face. That was when tears began to flow.

Chub disappeared for almost two weeks after Earle left for Marine Corps training on his way to the war in the South Pacific. No one could find the dog around the farm. He returned two weeks later—thin but ready to help with the usual farm chores. Two years later, when Earle returned to Scarborough to heal from his wounds, Chub was among the first to greet him, ready to help with his recuperation.

When Earle and Winonah married on November 26, 1946, Chub came along as part of the package. Nonie tried to train Chub to stay outside, but Chub had other plans. He started limping. Nonie, worried, thoroughly examined him, brought him into the house to nurse him, and kept the old dog comfortable. This went on for days, as Nonie tried to coax Chub to stay outdoors, he began limping for no apparent reason, and she brought him inside to care for him.

The limping stopped as soon as Earle's truck came into the driveway. Chub came to life, tail wagging as he bounded happily to greet his master. Nonie just raised her hands and declared, "I give up!" Thus Chub secured his place in the home.

Chub was there to greet Earle and Nonie's firstborn son, Philip, in September 1947. The old dog died peacefully in the spring of 1949 around the time daughter Earlene (Kitty) was born. Earle said goodbye to his dear devoted friend and laid Chub to rest in a plot on the family farm.

CHAPTER 8
Beech Ridge Community School

Chub attended school only one year, though he was welcome any time. He had proved his value in helping the teacher keep order. The following year the older, more disruptive boys had moved on to be part of the Conservation Corps.

As the years passed Florence and Earle took on more duties as older students themselves. Bright students like Florence often had the task of being mentor-readers who helped younger students develop their reading skills. Because illness kept Florence from attending school the better part of one year, she had to get a clean bill of health from Dr. Wentworth and was required to pass certain school tests before she was allowed to return. She aced the tests since she had studied on her own at home using books her mother had borrowed from the Westbrook library; consequently, Florence skipped two grades in school and became a big help to the teacher with struggling students.

Capable boys, like Earle, were often selected to arrive a bit earlier and build the fire in the wood stove that heated the large classroom. They also had the duty of carrying a five-gallon pail to Beaver Brook (about a mile away) and filling it with fresh brook water. This supplied drinking water for the children.

Earle soon discovered that in the spring this was a particularly fine duty to pull, and he often volunteered. He had discovered that trout were abundant in the spring. So, pocketing a fish line before leaving for school in the morning, he headed off with his friend Paul Robinson to fill the five-gallon pail with water—and participate in a little extracurricular activity as well. He quickly dropped the line into the water hole as he used the current to fill the pail with fresh water. Shortly, he had fish on the line and snapped it back in. Bundling the caught fish in a newspaper, he carefully deposited the package under a cool bush to retrieve later. Then the boys headed back to school with the water supply. Whenever the water level dipped, they were quick to notice and attend to the need. At the end of the day he raced to Beaver Brook to collect his catch of the day and brought it home for supper.

Beech Ridge Community School was indeed a "community "school. During the 1930s, when money was often hard to come by, many families worked for the school to help defray their yearly tax payments. Some cut and split wood to supply fuel for the wood stove, the only means of heat in the building. Other families cleared snow to keep the school accessible. Each family helped out where they could.

Florence and Earle always brought extra food in their lunch pails to share with fellow students who had little or nothing for their meals. Living on a farm that had large gardens and farm animals required work, but at least no one was in danger of going hungry. Mama and Dad taught their children to share with those less fortunate and not to judge.

The Community Club met at the school building on weekends, and families learned how quickly circumstances could change in a neighbor's health and ability to provide for their own needs. So they all looked out for each other and always tried to encourage those who were down.

Beech Ridge Community School

36

CHAPTER 9
Beech Ridge Community Club

In the late 1920s several families got together and decided to form the Beech Ridge Community Club. The initial goal was to improve the community and to bring electricity to the area. The Ahlquist family already had telephone service, but electricity did not arrive in the area until enough families became subscribers to Cumberland County Power & Light to justify running electric lines into the area.

Bertha Emerson and Mama (Marjorie Ahlquist) became primary workers for this cause. Bertha became president of the club, and Mama became secretary and treasurer. Members decided that every Saturday night during good weather the community would gather at the school-house. It became a Saturday night community dinner, featuring baked beans, casseroles, and pies. There was no charge, and people brought only their best offerings of food. The variety was wonderful.

Those who weren't on clean-up duty often played a card game called "63." Storytelling became a big attraction as did a good-hearted competition of "who could eat the most pieces of pie." Generally most boys could manage to eat about eight pieces of pie! Earle's favorite pies always included custard, lemon meringue, or fruit.

The gathering was intended as a good time and a chance to build community spirit. If a neighbor was in need, community members shared the burden and took measures to alleviate the stress. When someone had health problems, members set up a schedule and neighbors signed up to sit with the patient, bring meals, or provide an extra load of wood for the wood stove.

Amid the jovial conversation, community members discussed local concerns and set goals to progress forward. They often traded ideas and services. They all knew that when one family was down with health concerns or a lost crop or a wayward child or loss of work, they could very be next with their own troubles. No one was immune to hard times.

Inevitably there was joy in getting together, and everyone felt their burdens lighten when they shared and laughed together. When they addressed challenges as a group, they often found solutions. Then they all celebrated their joint success! As part of this effort, the community organized a voluntary fire department.

At the end of the gatherings, the Ahlquist family piled into the wagon with Dad and Mama seated in the front, the children and Chub in the wagon bed along with the cleaned, but now empty dishes. Flonnie asked Mama about the new family who had moved back into the area.

"Althea told me they were poor, Mama. She said they were all living with their grandparents. Is that right? And they seem sort of mean at times," Flonnie said.

Mama replied, "Sometimes hard times fall on families. You have seen us have some tough times, too. So you know it can happen to any of us. But we try to understand and never make fun of them."

Then Dad added, "Sometimes when people are scared, they act like bullies. Like a cat that puffs up to look big when it isn't. We don't make fun of them, but we don't give into them."

"Like when Chub went to school with me because big boys were acting like bullies?" Earle asked.

"Exactly," replied Mama. "We try to understand, we don't give into what's wrong, and we try to help in a way that helps and doesn't hurt their pride."

That evening, as the children got ready for bed, Mama recited a poem she had learned many years ago by Margaret Elizabeth Sangster.

The Sin Of Omission
by Margaret Elizabeth Sangster

It isn't the thing you do, dear,
It's the thing you leave undone
That gives you a bit of a heartache

At setting of the sun.
The tender work forgotten,
The letter you did not write,
The flowers you did not send, dear,
Are your haunting ghosts at night.

The stone you might have lifted
Out of a brother's way;
The bit of heartsome counsel
You were hurried too much to say;
The loving touch of the hand, dear,
The gentle, winning tone
Which you had no time nor thought for
With troubles enough of your own.

Those little acts of kindness
So easily out of mind,
Those chances to be angels
Which we poor mortals find—
They come in night and silence,
Each sad, reproachful wraith,
When hope is faint and flagging,
And a chill has fallen on faith.

For life is all too short, dear,
And sorrow is all too great,
To suffer our slow compassion
That tarries until too late:
And it isn't the thing you do, dear,
It's the thing you leave undone
Which gives you a bit of heartache
At the setting of the sun.

CHAPTER 10
Paving the Way for Electricity

Oak Knoll Farm was aptly named. It not only stood on the crest of a hill, it was surrounded by massive oak trees that bordered the dirt Beech Ridge Road in Scarborough. Though community members dearly loved their rural setting and the big protective trees, they were also anxious to be part of the progress enjoyed by their neighbors in the rest of Scarborough and nearby Gorham and Westbrook. It was an ever-present topic at the Beech Ridge Community Club and the Saturday night gatherings.

Though most farms in the area depended upon horse and sled or wagon for transportation, several households had an automobile, which was considered a good-weather-only means of transportation. One thing that limited automobiles was the condition of the roads. The 1910 Town Reports cited an Article proposed to consider limiting the speed of automobiles to eight miles per hour because 10 miles per hour was considered excessive. Gasoline cost about 14 ½ cents per gallon in 1912; in 1924 a Model T Ford sold for $240. The Ahlquist family owned a car, but they put it up on blocks in the winter to save the tires. It still proved useful, however. A belt was hitched to the axles so that the car engine could be used to power a saw blade to cut wood.

After Albion Ahlquist (Dad's older brother) replaced Libby's Bridge over the Nonesuch River in 1927, the Community Club thought they were on the way to making progress. The bridge was built with local labor using hand carts, oxen, and horse-drawn wagons. The community finally had more direct means to get to Coal-Kiln Corner of North Scarborough and Gorham and Westbrook. It clearly was an improvement over the very rickety bridge that spanned the river before the construction. The new bridge saved travelers a lot of time.

40

The community club lobbied for electricity and got it in 1931 when Cumberland County Power & Lights installed electric power in the area. The community felt this was a big step toward progress. But before the electric lines could be laid, the condition of the roads had to be addressed. As early as 1927 when approval and funds were in place for Uncle Al to replace the Libby Bridge, the topic of road paving was on the local agenda. The community determined that the road construction had to be done in several stages, some of which would be the responsibility of local residents. The electric poles had to be in place before the road could be paved. That required the removal of the massive oak trees that stood on either side of the road, reducing the width of the road to that of a wide lane—not quite wide enough to accommodate electric poles.

Community members held meetings to ponder how to accomplish the task safely. Most agreed that the beautiful old oaks needed to be removed, but they were so big (some more than three feet in diameter), people noted that would be extremely difficult to remove the trunks once they had been cut down with saws and axes. There was a lot to ponder.

Neighbor Harry Libby's father-in-law, Mr. Tracy, was head of the nearby correctional facility and experienced in tree removal. When the topic was raised at the Saturday night social, he proposed a solution. Mr. Tracy suggested drilling holes every 20 feet in the trunks once the trees had been felled and filling the holes with gun powder. (The gun powder was readily available in North Scarborough at an old abandoned factory). Then the powder would be lit, and the force of the explosion would splinter the massive stumps.

The community embraced the proposal. On a mild day in 1929, the trees were cut and the holes drilled and filled with the explosive. After everyone backed away a safe distance, the powder was ignited. The resultant blast blew the big oaks apart.

What an eventful day! Earliest among Flonnie and Earle's recollections was the memory of weeding the garden with their mother when they heard loud "BOOMS" as the trees fell and were then blown apart. With their beloved trees removed, the paving could progress. Another big step forward.

Farmers chopped up the chunks for fire wood and carted it away.

Then workers removed what remained of the stumps or cut them to make the ground as level as possible, laying the groundwork for the paving of Beech Ridge Road.

The community aimed to accomplish the paving before 1931, when the electric installation was scheduled. Paving the road after the trees had been removed required a three-stage process. Earle was fascinated by it. The road had been smoothed as much as possible by all the residents along their stretch of road. Once that was accomplished, a 500-gallon tank truck filled with liquid tarvia arrived, and the material was poured through pipes onto the roadbed. This was followed by a few truckloads of sand. Men stood on the back of the trucks and spread the sand over the tarvia. The third stage involved dragging gray birch branches across the sand. Like gentle rakes, the tree tops spread the sand, distributing it evenly over the tar.

It all seemed perfectly amazing to Earle.

The paving was completed in time; then, and only then, did the Cumberland County Power & Light Company consider the neighborhood had met the specifications to install electric power to that end of town. In early summer of 1931, the company installed electric poles to which electric lines would be placed. By August of 1931 the Ahlquist farm finally was wired for electric service.

With the advent of electricity, members of the Beech Ridge Community felt that they now met the standard of living enjoyed by the rest of the town. It was a milestone to celebrate!

CHAPTER 11
The Day Electricity Came to the Farm

Though a Maine mill installed the state's first electric light in 1880, more than 50 years would pass before Oak Knoll Farm became wired for electricity. Earle was five years old, Flonnie was seven, Edward was two, and Leroy ("Lee") was just six months old. Two neighbors, Fuller Merry and Lawrence "Pete" Storey, came to wire the old 1750 farmhouse. Dad took Edward to the barn to help him there, while Mama busied herself in the summer kitchen. Florence had charge of caring for baby Leroy, and Earle served as a helper to Pete and Fuller.

Pete worked in the cellar installing a fuse box and channeling armored cables (two wires sheathed in a metal casing) through the rooms of the upper stories of the house. He entered the cellar through a trapdoor in the parlor, which he inadvertently left open. Fuller enlisted Earle's help to spot the wires as they emerged through the walls or from the floors. In between times, Earle became Fuller's go-fer to locate needed tools. Earle loved it.

Flonnie put Leroy in the baby carriage, cooed to him, and wheeled him around the house. Intent on telling baby Leroy a story as she jiggled the carriage in the parlor, Flonnie stepped backwards and then let out a scream as the carriage upturned and she and the baby fell through the open trapdoor.

Fortunately, Pete was working just below them. Hearing the shriek, he quickly turned and stepped over in time to catch baby Leroy as Flonnie tumbled to the dirt floor. Pete just chuckled as Flonnie righted herself. He patted the baby, who squealed with delight.

"It seems he likes flying, Missy," Pete said as he winked at Flonnie, handed her the infant, then efficiently returned to his work. A stunned

Florence took baby Leroy, laughed herself at her dimpled brother, then took the stairs to go back to the parlor.

When things settled down and Fuller announced to Mama that the work was nearly complete, Mama climbed into the Model T Ford and drove to Westbrook to buy the family's first electric radio, three table lamps, and several bulbs at the Tic-Tock Jewelry Shop.

The arrival of electricity was a momentous occasion at the farm. Everyone sat down after they finished their chores and listened to the new radio. One could shut the lights off by merely pulling a string. The oil lamps were stored high in the pantry. The house no longer smelled of oil, nor did Earle or Flonnie have to trim wicks and clean the globes nightly. It would be years before the family had an electric stove or electric appliances, but to have a radio and electric lights brought joy to everyone in the family.

They particularly prized the electric radio. No longer did Dad and Pa become frustrated as they tried to listen to a ball game or Dempsey fight only to have the old battery-operated radio reception falter. Now they could sit with their pipes stoked, concentrate on the game, and feel as if they were almost there!

The radio became a staple. It connected them to the larger world beyond the farm and their close-knit community. Favorite programs included President Roosevelt's "fireside chats," ball games, story hours, and music. In the mornings Ken McKenzie and Montana Slim and other country singers performed over the air. In the early evening all the children hurried through their chores so they could listen to "The Shadow," Jack Benny, Fibber McGee and Molly, George Burns and Gracie Allen, or Amos and Andy. Soon the children began improvising and acting out some of the stories they heard on the radio during play time. Such wonderful, silly times they had!

Mama liked the music. Dad liked the ball games, news programs, and farm reports. All the children enjoyed the story programs.

Mama and Dad shook their heads and smiled. They weren't too sure their children needed more imagination, but they felt sure the radio had brought a much larger world into their home.

CHAPTER 12
The Greenhouse

The 1920s was a hopeful time for the family. Even though there were real setbacks and concerns, on the whole Mama and Dad were optimistic. They were one of the few families in the neighborhood who had a telephone; they had a solid old farmhouse and were making steady home improvements; they had dear family and friends nearby; they had two healthy children—Florence and Earle—and even though a set of twins were born prematurely and died, that terrible sadness did not dampen the joy they felt knowing they were expecting another addition to the family in 1929. And though there were rumblings of unrest in Europe, the family believed that those events were far away and would not touch America or cousins in Norway. Given all that, Dad decided to explore the possibility of building a greenhouse to increase the productivity of the farm. And Dad knew exactly who to talk to, John Libby.

John walked over the land with Dad. Together, they determined the best location for the 20' x 30' greenhouse would be the south side of the land on a nearly flat terrain. They secured the needed materials: storm windows, studding, copper tubing, a coke burner for heat, building materials for seedling trays, and screening for loam. They bought used materials whenever possible.

As summer approached in 1929, Ma spent more time at the farm to help Mama with tasks. Mama needed to be especially careful with this pregnancy because she had lost the twins the year before. Flonnie tried to be as helpful as possible. She was excited about starting school that coming September. Mama made Flonnie's school clothes, for the most part using the pretty printed cotton grain sacks that could be repurposed into children's clothes by clever home sewers like Mama. She proved to be especially clever in creating reversible shirts and blouses. When the clothes got soiled, the wearer could turn them inside out and no one could tell because of Mama's carefully finished seams.

With the new baby's birth day drawing near, Ma and Flonnie helped Mama put up jams and jellies and canned produce that was in season. They set as their goal 700 quarts for the winter, including food that would not be processed until after the last of the harvesting in the fall. But it was important to get under way as soon as they could.

At the end of August, Dad phoned Dr. Stickney from Saco with the news that Mama was about to give birth. Ma came to help as well. She had attended Mama when the twins were stillborn the year before. Leaving Mama in those capable hands, Dad and Earle went to visit John Libby and discuss more details about the construction of the greenhouse. Edward August Ahlquist was born soon after, in August 1929—thankfully a very healthy boy. Mama, though weak, was recovering.

Edward was born with a protruding navel, which was remedied by placing a silver dollar over the navel and tying it in place with a belly band. He never needed corrective surgery and grew to be a healthy, strapping boy. Flonnie kept busy in the house as Mama's helper until she started school a few weeks later in September.

The greenhouse was built that fall. Neighbors and brothers all lent a hand in the construction. Earle kept busy either sifting loam through screening or running for tools. Everyone worked steadily on it throughout the fall and winter so that it was in full operation by the following year.

Dad and Earle drove to Clark's Hardware in Gorham and bought coke as fuel for the used copper-jacketed burner John Libby had located for Dad to purchase. The burner weighed close to 200 pounds and stood about four feet high with a diameter of almost 18 inches. Attached to the coke burner was a water pump that pushed heated water through 2½-inch pipes situated around the inside perimeter of the greenhouse. These pipes were raised slightly off the dirt floor in six rows, evenly spaced to heat the greenhouse. The boys and men built bedding and work trays for the seedlings. These were set at a working level and measured about 3 to 3 ½ feet in depth. The gaskets attached to the water pump had to be frequently adjusted—a challenge because of the danger of burns. It was all too easy to burn tender skin when steam escaped, so great care had to be taken.

Dad's birthday was the end of March, about the time when he poured over seed catalogs with a pencil and paper in hand, calculating how much seed to buy. The family not only bought seeds for their own extensive gardens, but they also sold seedlings to others who wanted to grow gardens. In addition, they sold fresh vegetables to city dwellers and pro-vided vegetables to Sher-

Dad with Nell and Dan getting ready to plant

man's store in exchange for things they could not grow. This was part of the area's barter/exchange economy when currency was scarce.

Early plantings were critical. Vegetables such as tomatoes, cauliflower, carrots, celery, chives, onions, cabbage, turnip, squash, and potatoes were staples in everyone's diets. But the farm grew herbs and flowers as well. Dad proved to be a good promoter. He posted pictures of the mature plants next to the seedlings, so that prospective buyers could see what the future held. The children spent hours cutting out pictures of the plants for these promotions. This was particularly effective with flowers like pansies. Earle, then later, Edward and young Leroy kept busy constructing wooden flats to hold the seedlings people bought.

The agriculture work did not stop with flowers and vegetables. Occa-sionally Dad took Earle and Edward into the woods to locate fruit or nut trees growing in the wild. There Dad deftly cut off a few branches, which he brought back to his trees and grafted onto his younger, healthy trees. The farm grew several varieties of apples including crabapples, pears, peaches, and cherries. Mama was one of the few people around who knew how to preserve crabapples; and of course she made wonderful jams and jellies. She had grown up on her grandfather's farm in North Waterboro, which had many acres of apple orchards.

The greenhouse proved to be a wonderful asset to the family for many years. Not only did it provide food for the family and produce to sell; but it also provided enough at times to give away to those in need.

Wild Strawberry Jam

Wild strawberries ripen in late spring. Wash and hull the best you can find. Put two layers in large ceramic bowl. Cover with equal amount of sugar. Let it rest 30 minutes. Transfer to large kettle and bring to a boil over low heat, simmering for 15 minutes. Pour jam into long shallow ceramic pan and cover completely with a glass. Set this in direct sunlight. Stir 2 to 3 times a day, taking care to prevent moisture from falling into jam. When sun no longer reaches jam, remove the glass top and again wipe moisture away. Keep in the pantry until the next morning. Place in sun each day until juice forms a jelly (about 2-3 days). Put in hot sterilized jars, seal, and store in cool place.

CHAPTER 13
Summertime and Coffee Breaks

The typical schedule of the farm included rising early—around 4 o'clock to feed and milk the cows and let the animals out to pasture. The family gathered for breakfast, packed school lunches, and began their day. The school-age children headed off to the schoolhouse. By 10 A.M. Dad would be due in from farm work for his coffee break, which usually included one of Mama's biscuits with her jam, a delicious cookie, or homemade doughnuts. The family could set their clocks by that 10 o'clock coffee break. It was a ritual.

Mama made coffee by pouring water to a certain stain line in a Fischer white enamel saucepan, bringing the water to a boil, tossing in about a handful of coffee grounds, setting the pan to the back of the stove to steep, then pouring steaming hot coffee through a strainer into a large ironstone mug. Topped with pure fresh cream from the favorite cow, and it was ready to be enjoyed with one of Mama's homemade goodies.

Dad's routine was like clockwork. After settling into his chair at the table, he poured steaming coffee into his saucer to cool, then carefully lifted the saucer and sipped the liquid as he enjoyed a homemade treat. He paused, filled his corncob pipe, and had a short smoke, enjoyed a bit of radio news, and looked over his calculations for plant rotation and care. Then, with a satisfied smile, he rose to proceed with the next task at hand.

Mama's Doughnuts
In good size bowl mix well: ¼ cup shortening (or lard), 1 cup sugar, 2 eggs, ½ teaspoon nutmeg, ½ teaspoons salt, 2½ teaspoons baking powder, about 4 cups of flour, and 1 cup of milk. Mix all really well

Earle, Dad holding Edward, and Flonnie, about 1930

and gently roll it out on a well-floured board. Cut with a doughnut cutter and deep fry in hot oil (375 degrees) until done. Remove from oil (after having turned it once) and drain on thick paper. To make chocolate doughnuts, add ¼ cup more sugar and 1 square melted dark chocolate. Oh so good!

All the family enjoyed this coffee break time as a midmorning pause in farm life. It matched the mid-morning recess at school, too, so it was easy to settle back into that routine when school ended and summer began.

In 1932, 1933, and 1934 coffee break time became a particularly favorite routine for young Edward to enjoy with his father while his older siblings were away at school. The same way Earle had been Rudolph's shadow before Earle started school, Edward followed his father about the farm doing chores, though much of the work had been done by Earle before he went to school.

During summer vacation, the children enjoyed playing on the home-made see-saw or packing picnic lunches and going to a nearby pond for a swim or blueberry picking at Aunt Georgie's blueberry plains or raspberry picking at their grandparents' home. And this often meant time with their cousins.

Blueberry picking was particularly good in the summer of 1932. Flonnie helped Mama prepare their picnic and pack baby Leroy's bag with all that would be needed. Earle climbed on the barrel he used to reach the harness for Fritz, readied the old horse, and drove the wagon into the yard to be loaded. They all climbed on board. Three-year-old Edward brought his push wagon to steady himself in the fields. Six-year-old Earle steadied the reins with ease as they headed out onto the road. Earle had been handling the horses for more than a year by then. Now he was a veteran, but it certainly helped that Old Fritz was gentle.

Driving down Beech Ridge Road as far as the Meserve house on the hill, Earle turned left onto a wood road and came out at Mitchell Hill Road. From there it was an easy pace to Burnham Road, where Aunt Georgie and Uncle Elton lived. The family started off early so as to beat the heat of day.

By 9 A.M. everyone was busy filling pails with luscious blueberries. Fritz had settled in the shade, and Chub remained close to Earle. Earle kept an eye on Edward and guided him and his wagon into a safe area to pick. As Leroy napped, Mama and Flonnie picked berries nearby, spelling Aunt Georgie or cousin Ginnie if Leroy awoke. Dad stayed home tending the weeding and care of the other animals.

About 10 o'clock they all needed a break and realized Edward was missing. Everyone called. No answer. Mama began feeling frantic; Georgie and Flonnie tried to keep everyone calm. Earle and Chub went into action. Earle figured that if he followed the trail through the woods left by Edward's little wagon, he could track down his little brother. And sure enough, he did. After about three-quarters of an hour—during which the rest of the family spent in stress and fear—Earle and Chub spotted the little tow-headed toddler deliberately pushing his wagon toward home. Edward had decided it was time for his coffee break with Dad, and he did not want to miss it!

Eddie's Blueberry Cake

2 eggs	1 tbls. baking powder
1 pint blueberries	1 c. milk with 1 teas. vanilla
3 c. flour	1⅓ c. sugar
½ teas. salt	⅓ cup butter

Dust flour over blueberries before putting in batter. Set aside. Cream together butter and eggs. Add baking powder. Then fold in milk and the rest of ingredients including the flour, adding the blueberries last. Lightly grease a rectangular pan. Pour batter in pan and sprinkle top with some sugar with nutmeg.
Bake at 350 degrees for 45-50 minutes.

CHAPTER 14
Challenges and Gaining Strength

A difficult winter followed a difficult summer and fall in 1933. A severe drought destroyed 22 acres of corn. Dad and Mama had been hopeful early in the year and even agreed to hire Maynard Meserve to help out at the farm for $1 a day. True to the agreement, Dad still paid Maynard. The drought was not anyone's fault. They would not go back on their word.

Then all the children had bouts of measles, chicken pox, and other childhood maladies. Mama was so busy caring for everyone else that she, too, became rundown and developed pneumonia. The doctor feared she would get tuberculosis. It was serious enough for her to go to the hospital. Ma tried all the home remedies she knew, but nothing seemed to work. Aunt Georgie, Aunt Lillian, and Ma tried to ease the load by helping with the chores now and then. But the workload fell mostly on Dad, Flonnie, and Earle because Edward and Leroy were still too young to be of much help. No one spoke of the gravity of the situation.

Aunt Georgie and her daughter Virginia stopped by early one afternoon. Virginia was the same age as Flonnie and it gave the girls time together as they helped do the laundry. Uncle Elton came by to pick them up after his work shift.

Aunt Georgie gave her brother an encouraging hug, saying, "We're praying, Bung [her pet name for Dad]. Remember, God looks over all of us and we look after each other." She turned to Flonnie and Earle with a smile and reminded Flonnie to read the bedtime stories. She told them she planned to come again the next day and asked Earle to come get her and Virginia in the wagon.

Flonnie and Earle put Eddie and Leroy to bed as Dad banked the fire in the kitchen. Coming back from the bedroom, Flonnie and Earle stopped at the kitchen doorway when they heard their father talking quietly. But no one was there, just Dad, and they heard him pleading and crying, saying, "Lord, I fear you are taking my Margie from us. She has the same pneumonia that killed her mother. Oh, Lord, don't let her die. The children and I need her so, and love her so much. Don't take her Lord, when her life is still needed here. Please, Lord, I beg You."

Earle and Flonnie stood very still and gripped each other's hands. Silently they walked close to Dad and took his hands in theirs and with tears rolling down their cheeks, they bowed their heads and joined their father in his prayer. He looked up and gathered them into his arms.

"We can help," Flonnie and Earle said simultaneously.

"And we won't say anything to the others. We can make it happen, Dad. And God will bring Mama home," said Flonnie. Earle nodded.

Dad gave a sigh. He indeed had very special children. If he had to, he knew he could pick up extra work painting with Oliver Milliken to help pay the medical bills. But he would have to rely on his two eldest children to keep the farm and the family stable. God willing, they would all make it, including Margie.

Mama did come home. She continued to struggle with health problems and often had to go back to the hospital. And each time the family came together. True to their word, Flonnie and Earle pitched in and did all that they could. Mama had taught them that they were never to waste their sorrows, but instead learn to use them, turning them into energy.

Many years later (as adults), Flonnie and Earle reflected on that time by saying they were expanded by love, and God blessed them as they made themselves available, enabling them to do extraordinary things— giving them guidance and friends who helped. Earle said that he never would have believed the two siblings could have done all that they did, but that God brought them through. They kept the family intact, when other families in similar situations often separated and their children were sent to temporary orphanages. That never happened to the Ahlquist family.

The workload at the farm often conflicted with regular church attendance. If children were sick or animals needed extra attention, riding to Elm Street in Portland, where the church was located, proved too difficult. Mama and Dad tried to make up for this as much as possible with songs and Bible stories, but it wasn't the same as getting together with their friends at church. The family believed, however, that as long as they had their faith and treated others with care and respect (and that included animals), God would bless them.

The family loved their church and missed it when they couldn't attend. Pa and Ma told of how the family had been part of the original group who had built the church back in 1874. Uncle Christian had carved the altar, and Ma's brother Andreas had laid the mason blocks where the church stood. Aunt Thora had embroidered the altar cloths. This was a holy place for the Ahlquist family.

In 1938 when Pastor Kenneth Torvik came to serve the church, Pa and Ma along with Uncle Pete and Aunt Harriet went to him with a proposition. They proposed that twice a month he travel to Scarborough and conduct afternoon church services at their house for family members. Pastor Torvik agreed, and 40 to 50 Ahlquists gathered at the house in Scarborough to attend afternoon church services every other Sunday. The worship service included music, Bible stories, preaching, and prayer. Some of the hymns were sung in Norwegian but most of the service was in English for the sake of the children and those who had married into the family. And of course there was always coffee and refreshments afterward.

The children learned a simple table prayer: "Come, Lord Jesus, be our guest. And let these gifts to us be blessed. Blessed be God, who is our bread; may all the world be clothed and fed."

CHAPTER 15
The Depression

Though the Ahlquist children at Oak Knoll Farm did not hear directly about any worldwide economic depression, they all gradually saw the effects within their community. Earle in particular recalled one specific event that struck him as noteworthy.

When Earle was about five, a well-dressed man named Mr. Davis from Westbrook (an owner of Day's Jewelry Store), came to the farm to look at a young first-calf heifer for sale. (A first-calf heifer is a young cow that has had only one calf.) When asked the cost for this heifer, Dad set the price at $125. Mr. Davis left, thinking the price too high.

Through the winter, money became increasingly difficult to obtain, and many people relied on a barter and trade system. Farmers brought produce (eggs, cider, vegetables) to local shops in exchange for goods available at those stores. Money became scarcer as more banks closed. Paper money had no value, and businesses began accepting only coins.

In the spring, Mr. Davis came back to the farm and asked Dad if the first-calf heifer was still for sale. Dad replied that it was. "How much?" Mr. Davis asked. "Fifteen dollars," replied Dad. The heifer was sold, and Dad was relieved.

At school, Florence and Earle noticed several new students. Families had moved back into the area and were now living on the farms where they had been raised. The young parents had lost their jobs at city factories that had closed. Several generations lived in one house. The Clarks, the Lathams, and the Colprits now had grown children and grandchildren in their farmhouses. The Beech Ridge Community School expanded to include about 45 students and used both rooms for classrooms.

When winter arrived, some students came to school with rags

wrapped around their feet because they did not have shoes to wear. Families who could shared what they had to supply the needs of those who had fallen on hard times. Though everyone was affected by the hard times, the whole community pulled together and looked out for one another. Through the Beech Ridge Community Club they developed a community support network that put into action the desire to hold each other together.

In 1933, Uncle Al assisted the extended family by giving his parents and each of his brothers and sisters a 50-pound bag of oat, wheat, barley, and rye he had ground and mixed together. Each family cooked with the mixture, usually making a nourishing hot breakfast cereal. It lasted the whole winter and tasted great with molasses or maple syrup. Ma said, "It had everything in it but the kitchen sink!"

In the fall Dad drove the team of horses and the wagon to the back apple field of a neighbor. He and the children old enough to work gathered bushels and bushels of fallen apples. Some of the apples were stored in the farm's cool cellar, others were made into apple butter or jelly to spread on Mama's biscuits. Dad delivered the bulk of the dropped apples to Mr. Libby, who turned them into vinegar, which Dad took to sell at Sherman's Store.

Mama's Apple Jelly

About 4 pounds of assorted apples (both tart and sweet)
About 5 cups of water
3 cups of sugar (more or less, depending on the mix of apples)
1 lemon
Cinnamon or rosemary

Rinse and clean apples, removing stems. Chop apples into halves and quarters (seeds and skins and all—to be removed later) and put in heavy pan and add water. Simmer about 45 minutes until apples are soft. Remove from heat and let cool. Stretch a cheesecloth over another big pot and drain the cooked apples over the cheesecloth, separating the liquid from the apples (or a sieve can be used). This process may take a couple of hours. A big spoon can be used to move the process along. Cool the liquid apples overnight. The next day simmer the liquid and slowly add chosen spices, lemon juice, and sugar. Continue simmering until mixture reaches 220 degrees or when the jelly hangs on a spoon and sheets down as the spoon is turned upside down. Pour the jelly into clean sterilized jars and top with melted wax before the covers are attached.

The family ate even the apple remnants they gleaned from the cheesecloth—except the seeds—though the boys always dared each other to eat those as well.

CHAPTER 16
Apple-picking Time

The whole family got involved in apple picking. Typical of farm work, picking apples became a "family project," and Dad and Mama turned the learning into fun. As finances continued to be difficult for everyone during the 1930s, the Ahlquists developed resourceful ways. Toward late summer and early fall, Dad heard that the Randall Orchard in Standish and the Dole Orchard in Gorham had bumper crops with not enough hands to pick the apples. So he loaded up bushel baskets and sturdy children, and off they drove in the Chevrolet truck to Gorham, then later to Standish. Mama packed a hearty picnic lunch.

Early in the morning, as soon as the farm animals were fed and cared for, the family headed off on its apple picking adventure. They set a goal of collecting as many dropped apples as they could, filling the bushel baskets to the top with fragrant red apples---Cortland, Liberty, McIntosh. Though they were supposed to collect dropped apples, occasionally adventuresome Earle or Edward pretended to be monkeys and "climbed" just a bit to grasp a particularly appealing specimen. They could almost taste the apple pies, apple jelly, and apple butter Mama and Flonnie would be making.

Dad had bigger ideas. He had seen how neighbor Harry Libby turned apples into profit by making vinegar and selling it. Harry supplied four stores, transporting vinegar in big barrels, which were set up in the shop. Neighbors filled their crock jugs with the vinegar from the big barrel. Harry collected his fee in store credits to obtain whatever he and his wife, Lula, needed from the shop. Dad knew vinegar was in demand—it was used in cooking, canning, preserving and even cleaning—and he wanted to earn his own store credits for the acidic liquid.

After a full day of collecting apples, the Ahlquist family headed home in time to care for the animals and enjoy a tasty supper. That evening at bedtime, Mama recited a poem from her childhood, "Uncle Nathan Shaw." It left everyone giggling [see Appendix]. The tired workers slept well that night.

The next day everyone sorted the apples. They set some aside for cooking; some were saved for eating; and some would be delivered to Harry Libby to convert into vinegar. What emerged were big barrels full of pure vinegar, which Dad would trade for the family's necessities. Harry received a portion of the apples as his share, and he did more with them than just make vinegar.

Soon the Ahlquists would be heading to the local North Scarborough Fair. The fair was in the field behind the Grange Hall across from Sherman's Store at Coal Kiln Corner. It was held the first part of September every year. The fair of 1930 had been special because Edward placed second in "most beautiful baby." The family did think he was unusually handsome with his ringlets of blonde hair and big blue eyes. First place that year went to a pretty green-eyed brunette named Winonah Bowley. This year the Ahlquist family planned to enter a big pumpkin in the vegetable category. The children were excited and eager to see the horse race, the oxen pull, and the draft horse competition.

When they arrived at the fair, Flonnie and Earle spotted their neighbor Harry Libby. He had a beverage stand advertising cider for sale. Under the sign was a second set of letters: "New Cider, three years old." A long line of men waited to buy the drink. (Prohibition was still in effect, and Mr. Libby's "cider" contained a high alcohol content, which made it illegal to sell.) The children turned to Mama with questioning eyes. She quickly explained, "We don't buy Mr. Libby's cider. It is definitely not for children, but could sometimes be used in medicine."

With so many activities at the fair, it wasn't hard to distract the children from the illicit cider. Four-H exhibits with pigs, calves, chickens, handmade goods, and prize vegetables soon caught their attention. Mama promised that they could join 4-H themselves when they were older and exhibit their own work. They dashed off to watch the horse race from Knight's Farm to the Grange Hall on County Road. Then Earle took part in the "pig scramble," where he had to try to catch a greased baby pig. Running as fast as he could, he managed to capture the wriggly pink pig, which he brought to his cheering parents. He named the pig Pinkie and brought it home that night. Pinkie soon kept company with Blossom and the other cows in the barn, and the pig's care and feeding were added to Earle's duties. Flonnie came home from the fair with ideas for sewing projects. Mama promised they would start on that soon. Flonnie's first project would be making a pretty apron.

Here is the recipe from Mama's grandmother for a strong homemade cough syrup.

Grammie Jayne's Cough Syrup

1 cup light corn syrup
1 cup sugar
1 pint vodka or hard cider
Several sprigs of peppermint

In heavy pan bring syrup and sugar to a boil to dissolve the sugar but not to burn. Remove from heat. Cool to lukewarm. Stir in vodka or hard cider and add peppermint. Store in a sterilized colored glass bottle with a tight stopper.

Grammie Jayne said this cough syrup had to be kept up high, away from husband and children, and whenever a spoonful was given to anyone, she advised mother to take a teaspoon herself.

This cough syrup wasn't used often; it was administered only to treat very bad coughs.

CHAPTER 17
Maple Syrup Time

In the late winter and early spring, when the weather was just right—below freezing at night and brisk but still warming during the day—it was time to tap the maple trees. Tapping trees for maple syrup had to take place before the leaves budded. Dad told Earle that the alternate freezing and thawing caused pressure within the tree to start the sap flowing. Only enough sap would be tapped to provide a good supply for the family but also to ensure that the tree had enough nourishment. When buds finally started to emerge to form leaves, it signaled the end of the tapping process. It took about forty gallons of sap to produce one gallon of syrup. The sugaring season lasted about four to six weeks.

A row of sugar maples ran along the southern border of Oak Knoll Farm. Snow still coated the ground when Dad first examined the trees. He showed seven-year-old Earle how to drill a hole and insert a special spout into the tree. The drill bit had to match the size of the spout that would be gently tapped into the tree. Spouts had a sturdy wire hook attached where a bucket hung. The spout had to go in at a slightly downward angle so the maple sap would flow and drip into the waiting bucket. A tree of about twelve inches in diameter was about forty years old and would receive one tap. Bigger, older trees might receive several taps.

Earle's job was to harness Fritz to the sleigh (then later the wagon) and make the rounds of the tapped trees with Chub at his side. Earle replaced the filled buckets with empty ones to collect more sap. He secured the hanging pails with wire to keep them in place. He placed wooden disks over the filled buckets to keep the precious sap from sloshing out of the pails as they made their way back to the farm, where Mama and nine-year-old Flonnie turned the farm kitchen into a sugaring house.

They built an intense fire in the wood stove, then poured the collected sap into a large kettle, which they placed over the flames. As the sap boiled, some of the liquid evaporated. The remaining sap was reduced into a caramelized syrup with hundreds of golden bubbles. Mama and Flonnie tested the syrup by dipping a big scoop into the golden liquid, carefully drawing the scoop up, and watching as the syrup slid off the metal scoop as it was tipped. When tipped just so, Mama told Flonnie, the syrup poured out like a sheet. That was when the sap had reached the needed 219 degrees to qualify as syrup.

The syrup making went on for four to six week. Earle replaced the pails every day, collecting the sap and transporting the filled buckets to the summer kitchen. Flonnie boiled down the sap for syrup as needed.

At the end of the season Earle carefully pulled the tap spouts, cleaned them, and put them away for the following year. Flonnie and Mama stored the fresh syrup in quart jars. Before washing the pans, they carefully removed the sugared residue by rolling cleaned sticks along the edges to make maple sugar candy for all to enjoy.

The entire family enjoyed the maple syrup. They poured it on pancakes in the morning and used it to flavor ice cream and cakes.

Mama's Pancakes

Sift together 1½ cups flour with 3 teaspoons baking powder, 2 tablespoons sugar and 1 teaspoon salt. Set aside. Melt about 3 tablespoons lard in fry skillet In small bowl beat 1 egg with 1 ¼ cup milk, Add this to dry ingredients. Mix well, then add melted shortening or lard last. Then pour into lightly greased skillet When bubbles appear on top of pancakes flip over and brown on opposite side. Serve with dobs of butter melted on top. Then top with homemade maple syrup. Yum!

Mama's Maple Surprise

Cook in double boiler: 1 cup rice in 2 cups milk. This needs to cook about an hour until done. Beat 1 cup heavy cream, adding ¾ cup maple syrup gradually as the cream begins to thicken. Fold this into the cooked rice and store in a cool place. Serve with a cherry on top if you want to make it look special.

Rolling the roads in the winter.

CHAPTER 18
A Winter's Challenge—1935

Mountains of snow fell on the farmhouse in January 1935, but inside the family stayed warm and secure. In the fall the men had banked bales of hay along the foundation of the house to add to the insulation in the cellar, where canned goods were stacked on shelves and raw vegetables lay in the root cellar. Mama had put up 700 quarts of vegetables. Dad, Earle, and Edward had loaded firewood in the adjoining shed for easy access to the house. Dad and Earle had strung ropes to the barn and other outbuildings so that during the blowing snow they could hang onto the rope and find their way to the barn to care for the animals.

Every winter Dad drove the Model T Ford into the shed. He jacked the car up off its tires to save them for spring. He put the sleigh in the place of the wagon to be ready to be pulled by the horses. When a blizzard struck, young boys, dressed for the winter chill, placed markers along the road edges to mark the path for the road crew. This prevented the road crews from veering off the roads as they packed down the fallen snow with the heavy rollers pulled by teams of horses. The boys knew these roads well. Often the crews were not as familiar with the slopes and turns of the roads and the boys' markers served as needed guides.

On January 18, 1935, the family prepared for a storm, which was predicted to hit the area. Dad and Mama listened to the farm report on the radio and carefully read the *Old Farmer's Almanac*. They were watchful, because Mama was expecting a baby, and her health was delicate.

In anticipation of the impending birth, Dad's mother and sister Ruth had come to the farmhouse to help. She and Ma had attended the births of the last two children. Ruth's fiancé, Dick Grant, came along as well, just in case he was needed. Dad fetched Dr. Stickney from Saco as Mama

Formal family portrait, 1936. Back row, from left: Flonnie & Earle. Front row, from left: Mama with Paulie, Dad holding Leroy & Edward

began having labor pains. Ma and Dr. Stickney assisted Mama, while Aunt Ruth and Flonnie started a stew cooking on the kitchen wood stove. Outside, the storm developed into a blizzard with blinding snow.

The children heard the birthing cry of their new little sister, Pauline Ruth Jayne Ahlquist—a beautiful sound. But Mama was having problems, and Dr. Stickney told Dad to ready the sleigh. Positioning the sleigh near the house, Dad packed warm blankets and heated stones wrapped in blankets, then carried Mama to the waiting sleigh as Dr. Stickney climbed in beside Mama. They sped to the hospital, leaving Ma in charge.

At Ma's instructions, Dick Grant put on snowshoes and headed to Westbrook to buy Karo syrup and evaporated milk to make a formula to feed baby Paulie. Well aware that the baby's life depended on him, he made it there in record time, carrying a backpack and covering ten miles.

Aunt Ruth telephoned her sister Harriet to tell her of the situation and ask for everyone's prayers. Anyone in the neighborhood who had a phone heard the news and added their prayers for Mama's recovery.

Mama spent several weeks in the hospital before she recovered enough to come home. She was still very weak, but God brought her home, of that the family was sure.

When Mama returned home she needed lots of help, so Ma, Aunt Georgie, and Aunt Ruth came to the farm to lend a hand. Flonnie and Earle stepped up even more to reduce Mama's stress. With Mama in bed much of the time, Flonnie became a little mama to baby Paulie. They both loved the arrangement, and it gave Mama more time to rest. Dad took on more outside work to help pay for the medical bills so he relied on Earle, Edward, and Leroy to pick up more of the farm's chores while still attending to their school work.

Mama continued evening stories or poems before bed. Many of the poems were from her childhood. One was a favorite from Annie Johnson Flint.

What God Hath Promised
By Annie Johnson Flint

God hath not promised skies always blue, Flower-strewn pathways, all our lives thro,'
God hath not promised Sun without rain, Joy without sorrow, Peace without pain.
God hath not promised We shall not know Toil and temptation, Trouble and woe;
He hath not told us We shall not bear, Many a burden, Many a care.
God hath not promised Smooth roads and wide, Swift easy travel, Needing no guide;
Never a mountain, Rocky and steep, Never a river Turbid and deep:
But God hath promised Strength for the day, Rest for the labor, Light for the way,
Grace for the trials, Help from above, Unfailing sympathy, Undying love.

The family knew they were blessed—they were together, surrounded by family and friends; Mama was gaining strength daily; and they had food enough to share, warm clothes, and a warm house. Dad and Mama reminded them spring was coming! Spring meant planting, in the greenhouse and then in the soil, and harvesting. Life was good!

CHAPTER 19
Rabbits and Moving Buildings

Among Mama's endeavors was her rabbit herd, raised for their fur, particularly angora and chinchilla rabbits. Their warm fur could be spun into fine yarn for knitting. The family raised, bred, and combed the rabbits to gather the fur. They also sold young rabbits. Since most women of the time knitted hats, sweaters, mittens, and scarves for their families, they prized this warm yarn, spun from the rabbit fur.

In May or June of 1935, Mama had returned home from the hospital and was still recovering from the challenging birth of Paulie, who by now was about five or six months old. Mama slowing gained back her strength, and all the children were trying to be helpful.

During this time, Earle was called over by neighbor Lula Libby to watch closely as Ira Dresser moved a small building across the field and nearer to the road. Since Harry Libby was somewhat deaf, Mrs. Libby wanted to make sure things were done right and asked Earle to report directly to her. Earle had often done odd jobs for Harry and Lula Libby, an older couple who lived across the road from the farm. Without getting in the way, nine-year-old Earle paid close attention to the moving operation. Earle not only reported the entire proceeding, including conversation and the final cost charged, to Mrs. Libby; but he also returned home with ideas about improving the family's own farm.

The moving project had given Earle an idea that he thought might prove beneficial for his mother, but he would need the help of his brothers. Walking about the farmyard, he measured things out in his mind, pacing out distances the same way he had seen Mr. Dresser do. Then he slept on the plan.

First thing in the morning after tending the chores, Earle turned to

Edward and Leroy, saying, "You know how Mama has her heart set on raising angora rabbits, but she's still not real well and can't walk that far?" Eddie and Lee nodded.

"Well, I know how we can move the old shed near the spring house up close to the barn. She can use it for her rabbits." Big grins flashed across their faces. They were in.

With Edward (age 6) and Leroy (age 4) nearby, Earle climbed on the barrel and harnessed the team of horses, Dick and Nell, who worked well together. Leading them forward, he attached a brace of skids to the team and drove them down near the spring where there was a vacant utility shed measuring about 16 feet by 20 feet. Using automotive jacks, the boys raised the building and eased the skids under it. Securing the back of the shed with strapping tied on both ends by chains and roping, Earle guided the team up the knoll near the barn, about 120 yards. Both Edward and Leroy marched alongside, alert to any slippage from the skids. They all eased the building in place, then tended Dick and Nell for the night. This was the Ahlquist boys' first building moving project.

Washing up, the boys went inside, quite satisfied with themselves. Mama's green eyes sparkled when they announced she now had a rabbit house close to the barn. When Dad came home, he sat down for supper, looked out the window where the big oak tree grew near the spring, and asked, "What happened to the shed?"

Earle, Eddie, and Lee just smiled at each other as Earle replied, "Oh, we moved it near the barn."

Mama added, "It's for my rabbits."

"Great, " Dad said. "It will be easier for you to get to."

Earle, Eddie and Leroy were especially tired when they climbed into bed that evening. It had been an eventful day. Instead of a bedtime story from a library book, Mama recited the words of a favorite song from her childhood. It was Earle's favorite as well. They all slept well that night.

The next day the boys began building separate pens for the different rabbits. With Dad's added job painting for Oliver Milliken and Mama's wool yarn business, the family gradually worked its way out of the medical debts that had accumulated after Paulie's birth. The whole family pulled together and kept a thankful spirit.

Two Little Boys

By Theodore F. Morse and Edward Madden

Two little boys had two little toys,
Each had a wooden horse,
Gaily they'd play, each summer's day,
Warriors both, of course;

One little chap then had a mishap,
Broke off his horse's head.
Wept for his toy, then cried with joy
As his young comrade said,

"Did you think I could see you crying
When there's room on my horse for two?
Climb up here, Joe, and don't be sighing,
He can go just as fast with two.
When we grow up, we'll both be soldiers
And our horses will not be toys,
Then I wonder if you'll remember
When we were two little boys.

Long years had passed, war came at last,
Gaily they marched away;
Cannon roar'd loud, 'midst the mad crowd,
Wounded and dying Jack lay.
Loud rings a cry, a horse dashes by,
From out the ranks of blue;
Gallops away to where Jack lay,
As a voice comes strong and true.
"Did you think I could leave you dying
When there's room on my horse for two?
Climb up here, Jack, we'll soon be flying,
To the ranks of the boys in blue.
Did you say, Jack, I'm all a-tremble?

Well, perhaps it's the battle's noise,
Or it may be that I remember
When we were two little boys."

Sherman's Store.

CHAPTER 20
Sherman's Store

Dad readied the wagon with Dick harnessed to the load. Together Dad and Earle rolled two big barrels filled with vinegar into the back of the wagon, being careful to secure them with rope so they wouldn't shift and throw the balance of weight off during the ride. Earle and Chub climbed aboard. Mama handed Dad a grocery list, then she carefully placed a basket of eggs in the back of the wagon. It was well-cushioned with soft flannel. She added several jars of her prized canned vegetables, also well-cushioned with extra flannel. Lastly she handed Earle two envelopes, all stamped and addressed. They were headed to Sherman's Store, which also served as the local post office.

It took about 30 to 45 minutes to travel to Sherman's Store by wagon. The vinegar barrels, eggs, and canned goods were like money in the bank. Traversing down the long hill and up Sand Hill, they had to negotiate carefully so as not to lose the load or overwork old Dick. Their pace was slow and steady. Dad carefully checked the wheels and wagon brakes before loading the wagon—going down Meserve's hill required skilled braking, and crossing Nonesuch River and going up Sand Hill put more pressure on Dick. Dad kept a canvas feed bucket handy as an inducement to Dick if there was any trouble.

Earle liked going with Dad to Sherman's Store, and he particularly liked Mr. Sherman. He relished the chance to learn news to report back to Mama and to pick out candy for sisters and brothers (a lot could be bought at one cent a piece, and he had two dimes in his pocket).

O. E. Sherman & Son store was located on County Road near the intersection with Saco Street (which was an extension of Beech Ridge Road), the area in North Scarborough known as Coal Kiln Corner. Joe

73

Sherman, Orra's father, had opened the store around the time of the Civil War in the 1860s. Joe was originally from York County, where he had served as York County sheriff. Dad told Earle that somewhere back there the Shermans were related to the Chadbourns in Waterboro, so perhaps that was why Orra and Will Sherman took a special interest in the Ahlquist children. The store was a hub of activity and an integral part of the community. It was diagonally across the road from the North Scarborough Grange Hall, where monthly meetings and the annual fair were held.

Safely pulling up to the back of the store, Earle had to situate Dick so he could enjoy a long drink of water. Then he took the canvas feed bag and gave Dick a well-deserved treat of new grain. Dad had already gone inside to notify Orra of their arrival. Orra and his brother Will came outside, and the three men carried the canned goods and eggs into the store. Then they carefully rolled the barrels of vinegar inside and deposited empty barrels into the wagon.

Inside the shop, Dad and Earle passed brightly colored cloth bags filled with grain and flour layered carefully on long tables. Orra opened his ledger book and entered the value of goods Dad had brought. That way Dad knew how much money he had on his account. He gave Orra Mama's grocery list, and Orra collected the supplies as Dad walked to the center of the store and watched Old Joe Sherman move his checker skillfully on the board, besting Ben Roberts with his move. Joe looked satisfied as he leaned back in his chair, but a twinkle came into Ben's eyes as he made a quick move that surprised the old man. They each grinned, and the game continued.

"How's Margie?" inquired Ben.

"Doing better, each day she is getting stronger," Dad replied.

With a nod of his head, Ben returned to the checker game. Ben had also grown up in Waterboro, where his father, Judge Roberts, had been Mama's guardian after her grandparents died. Because of this connection, Ben too, had a special interest in the Ahlquist family.

Earle went to a big table near the back and pulled out all the mail addressed to his household and to the neighbors; then he carefully took Mama's two letters and handed them to Mr. Sherman behind the counter.

Only then did he take a long look at the penny candy arrayed under the glass counter. Carefully fingering the two dimes in his pocket, Earle carefully selected his twenty pieces of candy. Mr. Sherman, with a twinkle in his eye, pulled out a small brown bag and filled it with Earle's selections. That completed, they each smiled and exchanged goods for money.

In the background, a country western song played on the radio. Earle wasn't paying close attention until he saw Mr. Sherman quickly walk over and shut off the radio, simply saying, "No one need hear about any one cheating on their partner. Times are hard enough, we need to encourage every family to stay together and help each other out."

The men around the checker table nodded in agreement. "That's right, Orrie," several of the men said.

 Quietly Joe added, "The man who walks with God will always arrive at his destination. Our job is to be signposts along the way." Another murmur of agreement rose from those gathered.

When Earle next looked up he saw that their vinegar barrels had been installed with a spigot, with jars nearby. Already, customers were lining up for the fresh vinegar. On the other side of the room a similar barrel contained molasses. Toward the front of the store a small, but similar barrel contained motor oil. At the front of the store, outside near the porch, cars pulled up to the two gas pumps, where customers could buy 12 gallons of gas for a $1.

After carefully packing up their purchases, Dad, Earle, and Chub headed back home, their task completed. They felt happy to have such good neighbors.

During the Depression, when so many families struggled financially, Sherman's Store remained an anchor for the community. Orra Sherman set up a barter system to allow families to trade their produce, vinegar, and eggs for the goods their families needed. Orra kept a ledger account book to keep track of the transactions. Everyone paid his or her own way---using trade and barter instead of cash. More than once the Sherman brothers extended short-term loans so that families could pay taxes and not risk losing their homes.

Orra, who was the proprietor, did not sell liquor. He attended church every Sunday and believed in living by his faith in his business as well as personally. No one used bad language at the store. It was a safe space to come. Everyone, including children, was welcome and treated with respect. People responded in kind.

CHAPTER 21
Sewing and Laundering the Modern Way

Soon after Leroy was born in 1931 and the farm was wired for electricity, Mama and Dad began to purchase modern conveniences. Though the Ahlquists, like much of the world, had to cope with an economic depression, they nevertheless felt hopeful. After all, they could now listen to the ballgame and Amos and Andy on the radio. They had electric power in their home, and they now lived on a paved road. Earle was particularly thankful he no longer had to clean the lantern globes of soot each night with old newspapers—a dirty job that seemed to take forever before he could finally crawl into bed. The family had land to grow their food, with a crop large enough to sell at market. They had healthy children; they had family, friends and a connection to their heavenly Father. They had love.

When a man from the Cumberland County Power and Light Company came to the farm to collect his monthly electric bill payment, he arrived in a handsome truck with a sign on the cab that exhorted, "Try one Free." The truck bed held a large copper barrel with a motor attached and a contraption that appeared to be a wringer—an Easy electric-powered wringer washing machine. He told Mama she could try it for free for one month to see if she liked it. If she didn't or if the family could not afford it, he would take it away at no charge.

Mama and Dad managed a tight budget, but they decided to give the machine a try. After reviewing the instructions, Mama figured she could make it work. The men deposited the machine in the summer kitchen, near the old galvanized basin that had been used for washing. Mama and Dad checked it over carefully. Of course, Flonnie and Earle, curious about the new contraption, had to examine it as well.

On Monday, after early morning farm chores were done, Mama packed Flonnie and Earle's school lunches with the usual extra for them to share. Flonnie had collected dirty clothes and deposited them in the summer kitchen, saying, "Do you think I should stay home and help you run this new washing machine, Mama?" Mama just smiled and replied, "No, you run along to school. I think I can handle this. I will let you know how it goes when you get back from school. And remember, we will start our sewing lessons soon. Promise!" With that, Florence and Earle headed for Beech Ridge School. Eddie accompanied Dad in the barn, and baby Leroy played on the floor near the sorted laundry.

With written instructions nearby, Mama systematically rolled the machine to transfer the heated water from the holding tank into the copper galvanized basin, then added the soap and dirty clothes. She plugged it in, turned it on, and watched in amazement as the machine spun and churned the dirty clothes. After the clean water rinse, she fed the clean clothes through the wringer. It amazed her how much drier the clothes were after going through the wringer. This allowed the clothes to air dry much faster than before. In no time at all, it seemed, she had clean clothes hanging on the line to dry. Washing the laundry by hand used to take her most of the day. Now, the entire household laundry was done before noon.

When Dad and Eddie came in ready for lunch, Mama had a bright smile on her face. "Rudolph," she said, "I think we have to find a way to buy this washing machine." She looked so pleased that he just smiled and brought out the pencil and paper to figure the numbers.

Flonnie and Earle returned home after school to a smiling Mama, who was collecting several loads of clean laundry from the clothes line. Flonnie helped unpin and fold the clothes as her mother exclaimed, "We are finding a way to keep that wonderful machine! And I am going to teach you to sew this very afternoon. We don't have to wait until tomorrow. This new machine has saved me so much time that we can start right now."

Mama and Dad moved a work table into the center of the summer kitchen, where Mama laid out scissors, pins, and the fabric from one of the grain sacks, a pretty flowered fabric. The fabric had been carefully washed and dried to prevent shrinkage and prevent the colors from running or "bleeding." Mama added salt and vinegar to the rinse water to ensure colorfastness.

Laying out the tissue pattern for a skirt on the fabric, Mama had Flonnie carefully pin the pattern and fabric together. Flonnie paid close attention to Mama's instructions. She picked up the scissors and cut the fabric, being careful not to damage the pattern so that it could be used again.

Mama had learned from her grandmother how to sew on a treadle sewing machine. This machine became Flonnie's instrument as well. Pulling up a chair next to her daughter, Mama showed Flonnie how the top and bottom thread was channeled through the tiny holes. Carefully guiding the fabric under the presser foot, Mama stepped on the floor pedal to activate the sewing machine. As the needle went up and down, she demonstrated the coordination between the pedal and the needle as it drew thread through the layers of fabric and sewed them together. Mama began a seam, then stopped and switched seats with Flonnie, so Flonnie could complete the seam. At the end of the seam, Mama left the needle in the fabric as she lifted the presser foot and carefully turned the fabric around. She then lowered the presser foot and showed Flonnie how to take a few more stitches in the fabric to lock the seam in place. After cutting the thread and removing the fabric from the machine, Mama let Flonnie examine her handiwork. "Wow," said Flonnie, "this is great. Let's show Dad." Mama smiled. Her daughter was on her way to becoming a seamstress.

Flonnie would soon be able to help with the family sewing, allowing Mama time to earn extra money herself doing alterations for Tom Tailor's Shop at Morrills Corner in Portland. That money could help pay for the new washing machine.

Later Mama bought an attachment to the treadle sewing machine that enabled her to run it using electricity. Mama taught neighbors Lillian Robinson and Muriel Merry how to do the same with their treadle machines. A few years after that, Mama and Dad bought a new portable Singer sewing machine—a dressmaker's model—that Mama and Flonnie used to make fashionable dresses that sold in specialty shops.

The Ahlquist women tended to be very capable with sewing machines and freely traded patterns and ideas with each other. Aunt Georgie had a steady stream of clients who hired her to sew for them regularly. The women in the family were noted for their skill in fitting patterns to various figures and making the garment look flattering. Mama's grandmother (Jayne Clough Chadbourn) was a noted seamstress in the Waterboro area.

Even everyday clothes were prepared with care, with finished seams so perfect that the garment could be worn inside out without detection. Few people noticed the shift because the inside seams were as finished as the outside ones.

By the time younger sister Paulie arrived in 1935, Flonnie had become a skilled seamstress. She loved to make Paulie outfits that matched her own, and Paulie delighted in wearing them.

CHAPTER 22
Sharpshooter on a Mission

When Earle joined the Marines in World War II and Edward and Leroy signed on with the Navy during the Korean War, they all qualified with ease as sharpshooters. The reason for their proficiency was simple—they had plenty of practice at home. On Saturdays when they had spending money, they walked five miles to Westbrook, meeting up with companions along the way, to watch cowboy movies at the Star theater. Roy Rogers and his horse Trigger and Gene Autry and Gabbie Hayes thrilled them with their on-screen escapades. The good guys *always* won on the silver screen, men treated women honorably, and language was clean and wholesome.

They often stopped at Karapus fruit store for snacks on their walk home, but they didn't linger too long. They knew they had to get back in time to get enough sleep to be able to rise at 4 the next morning to do their farm chores of caring for the animals. If they overslept, they knew restrictions would follow. The boys were careful to watch out for each other, too. They considered the rules both clear and fair.

The wonderful stories shown on the movie screen fueled the imaginations of the brothers. They started honing their skills with homemade slingshots, aiming at the open slats in the chicken coop. The brothers selected strong sapling branches with just enough spring to attach the homemade leather and an elastic strap to ensure accuracy in shooting. Squirrels became good moving targets. The boys eventually planned to target weasels, which often attack the farm's chickens.

Those western movies fed the brothers' sense of adventure and resourcefulness. With all the wild game around the farm, Earle soon discovered he could sell the animals' furs for very good money. Sam Scott had informed Dad that a fox fur pelt would bring a whopping $10 to $12. Average wage for a day's work was only $1.25—so the return on a fox fur pelt was pretty dazzling.

The challenge for a hunter, though, was that he had to shoot the animal dead without damaging the fur. Instead of using a gun, Earle decided to start by trapping animals and became proficient with a sling shot. With Chub nearby, Earle wandered the farm and learned the special places where foxes located their dens. Knowing that foxes were particularly fond of robbing the family's chicken coop, Earle had an extra incentive to capture the animals.

Fortified with advice from Uncle Toy, Dad, and Sam Scott, Earle made his first foray into trapping. Accompanied by Chub, Earle cautiously approached the foxes' den area and discovered the trail the animals followed to rob the chicken coops. Stealthily he placed the first trap, being careful to remove his scent as much as possible so as not to alert the fox. It took only a few days for Earle's efforts to succeed. Dad showed Earle how to skin the fox, preserving the pelt as much as possible. Then Sam Scott helped Dad and Earle redeem the pelt for $10.

That success launched eight-year-old Earle into business. Five-year-old Edward watched closely so that he could emulate his older brother. Dad and Mama, proud of their resourceful son, quietly discussed the possibility of buying a rifle for Earle. But that would come later. In the meantime, the boys used their imaginations to pursue their cowboy and Indian adventures.

House rules always applied. Only after chores were completed could the cowboys and Indians emerge. The fact that Oak Knoll farm had a hiding place from Indians in the closet next to the fireplace heightened the drama. The center chimney was designed so that crawling into the closet gave access to brick stairs that led to the roof, where a boy could lie and not be seen by attacking Indians.

Because access to that hiding place was in the parlor, the brothers often found themselves being shooed out of the house by Mama and Flonnie. Why those women never seemed to understand the importance of the cowboy and Indian drama, the brothers did not always appreciate. Urging her daughter to maintain a sense of humor, Mama quietly spoke to Dad and they developed a plan.

It wasn't long before Mama and Dad decided Earle could be trusted with more responsibility. They purchased a used .22 rifle, and Dad taught Earle the rudiments of handling it safely—complete with appropriate restrictions. Dad had been in the Army in the Great War as had Uncle Toy. He knew his way around guns even if he chose not to go hunting often. Dad reported to Mama that Earle was showing good understanding, so Mama told 10-year-old Earle on Saturday morning that she would appreciate a pheasant for supper that evening. Happy to rise to the occasion, Earle took the twenty-two and his trusty companion

Heroes that inspired: The Great War soldiers Peter Johnson, Rudolph, and Toy Ahlquist

Chub and they headed for the woods. Proceeding quietly, Earle described their task to Chub as he envisioned the Old West.

Before long both hunter and dog stopped dead still. Earle gave a hand signal to Chub, and the dog sprang into action, flushing out the pheasant from the junipers. Kneeling to aim, Earle raised the rifle, took aim quickly, and pulled the trigger. Down the pheasant came, and Chub retrieved the bird.

It wasn't long before young Earle could shoot the head off a pheasant at 200 feet. Aiming at the head prevented the bullets from lodging in the meaty part of the bird. He and Chub were quite a team.

Edward and Leroy watched this activity with interest. Though they still understood the house rules, the boys tended to let their imaginations lead them to adventures that were riskier than their parents wished. The boys found among Dad's tools in the shed a 20-gauge shotgun that was fitted with a "Damascus' barrel, which needed specific ammunition. Not thoroughly understanding that requirement, the adventuresome brothers decided to test out the new weapon. Putting the only ammunition they had into the chamber, they went to the field to aim at a target. With deliberateness Earle shouldered the shotgun and took aim as the younger brothers stood back and watched. Pulling the trigger, Earle got an incredible kick and shock as the gun barrel splintered, curling into a fan shape. The brothers dropped to the ground as they watched Earle massage his bruised shoulder as he set the 20-gauge down and they all considered what to do next and how they would tell their father. Straight talk with Dad was the only talk acceptable. They knew he would be understanding, thankful no one was hurt, and fully expected them to handle things respectfully and learn from their experiences.

The brothers conferred. Edward and Leroy immediately remembered the Wild West movies. What would Roy Rogers or Gene Autry do? A decision was made. They headed for the workroom. Securing the shotgun with the vice grip and firmly holding a hacksaw, Earle sawed off the damaged part of the barrel. Removing the shotgun carefully, the boys blew away the residual shavings and wiped it with a cloth. They had converted it into a sawed off shotgun just like Gabbie Hayes! Then to test it. They decided to maintain caution and care. Looking around they selected a strong young sapling with a good crooked branch. They mounted the 20-gauge into the crook of the tree, securing it with rope. They then tied a string to the trigger. Loading the gun, they stayed back a safe distance and together they pulled the trigger. It fired fine! What a relief! It certainly was a learning experience. But learn they did! The shotgun was seldom used, but there was a certain delicious joy in knowing they had one!

That evening after explaining the situation to Dad, he just smiled, saying, "Well, no one got hurt and you definitely learned something from it. Good enough!"

But as the brothers got older their mother could often depend on them for pheasant or fox for supper. She always managed to be a proficient cook. Few people would have guessed it was wild game.

CHAPTER 23
Mastering Important Subjects

Because of Earle's exceptional ability in math when he was a teen, one might assume he always loved math. But that wasn't true.

When he was in early elementary school, Earle had trouble learning his math tables. Instead of working on the math problems assigned by the teacher or Mama, Earle spent his time romping with Chub or playing cowboys and Indians with younger brothers in between farm chores. Listening to radio programs heightened the boys' desire to pretend they lived in the Wild West. Earle loved to pretend he was hiding from Indians in the secret cubby near the fireplace and then burst out to fight the bad guys. On nice days the seesaw held its own temptations. Math tables could wait, Earle figured.

Mama had other ideas. She invited cousin Dorothy (Uncle Al & Aunt May's daughter) to visit one Saturday. A rugged girl, Dorothy excelled in her classes at the high school. Mama was determined that this would be the weekend that Earle learned his math tables.

Mama turned to Dot and said, "Earle needs to master his math tables and don't hesitate to do whatever you need to do to make that happen." With that, she left the two of them alone in the parlor and herded the other children out of the area.

Earle, realizing that Dot would not hesitate (and might even relish) enforcing the lesson in ways he didn't want to experience, decided it was time to get down to business and learn those math skills. By the time the weekend ended, Earle had mastered those math tables and could demonstrate his learning Monday morning in class.

It wasn't long before math became one of his primary strengths as he found ways to use his skill in calculating logarithms, drafting, financial

Enjoying a ride on the seesaw, from left: Earle, Edward, Leroy, Paulie, and Flonnie, 1935/1936.

tables, square roots, and complex problem-solving related to calculus. These came in handy when he bought and sold wood lots and had to calculate timber board feet, move buildings, construct complex roofs, or build stairs.

It was no surprise that while still in high school, Earle was often called upon to be the substitute math teacher when the regular teacher was absent. His love affair with math had not been "love at first sight," but it endured once he understood its importance.

CHAPTER 24
Learning to Master Needlework

Florence tried hard to be Mama's dependable helper; on the whole, she stepped forward and was a quick learner, as she was in school. But try as she (and Mama) might, Flonnie just couldn't seem to master knitting and crocheting. Mama didn't understand why her very bright daughter, who was capable in so many ways, was a complete failure when it came to needlework. Flonnie genuinely seemed to want to learn, so it was not a case of willful stubbornness. Both mother and daughter were close to tears more than once during these lessons.

Convinced there had to be a better way, Mama contemplated the situation. She did not want her young daughter to grow up with a sense of failure in this most basic of skills. Mama knew that if Flonnie could master needlework, it would increase her sense of competence when faced with other manually demanding tasks. Admittedly, Mama thought, Flonnie might never enjoy or draw comfort from creating useful items in this way, and that was okay. But Mama could not imagine not being able to do needlework at all. She remembered the joy and sense of peace she gained when her grandmother had taught her how to knit, crochet, and sew, and she dearly wanted to pass that along to her own daughter. There had to be a way.

After perhaps the fifth attempt to teach her young daughter how to hold and work knitting needles—attempts that again and again ended in tears—Mama threw up her hands and said, "Okay, let's gather our books for the library. Today is the day to return them." With the children in tow, they piled into the car and headed to the Westbrook library. While driving there, Mama had an idea and determined to check it out with the librarian. When they arrived at the library, they proceeded to the desk,

Mama teaching neighborhood women how to tat around linen handkerchiefs in 1941. Flonnie is standing in back; Mama (with white hair) is seated in back in front of the open window.

and Mama instructed the children to select two books each. Resting her hand on Flonnie's shoulder, she gently held her back, saying to the librarian, "Do you happen to have a book on learning how to knit?"

"Why yes," replied the librarian, who guided them to that section of the shelves. Mama and Flonnie selected a book. Smiling, Mama nodded and directed Flonnie to go to the children's section to look for a book just for fun.

Perhaps, just perhaps, Mama thought, Flonnie could learn from a book, since books seemed important to her and had proven to be such a source of success in so many other areas of her young life. After all, God had created a wild assortment of flowers; none were the same. Perhaps people had different ways of learning. They would see.

And so it was that Flonnie became a proficient knitter by reading instruction books. She learned to crochet and tat in the same way—though tatting was especially difficult.

Mama watched her daughter steadily learn these skills. Together they celebrated when Flonnie presented her father with a warm scarf, and Dad proudly wore it.

It amazed Mama that her daughter learned this way, and that even though she could teach many others the arts of knitting, crocheting, and tatting, she could not communicate it to her own beloved daughter. But they had broken through the frustration and accepted their differences. Mama now had a sure helper to make hats, mittens, scarfs, and sweaters for family and friends to warm them through Maine winters. Flonnie, too, experienced the joy of making something useful and beautiful for herself and others to enjoy.

It wasn't unusual to see all three boys seated near the kitchen wood stove in the winter, along with their mother and sister, all knitting. Mama had little trouble teaching her sons to ply those needles with some skill. She always chuckled that she had been unable to teach her eldest daughter the art of needlework but had succeeded in teaching it to the boys and her youngest daughter.

Mama often looked at Flonnie as she worked on her latest needlework creation, shook her head, and smiled, amazed that her daughter could so easily read and interpret designs from a book, when that was exactly the thing so many found difficult. That was one mystery she could easily leave in God's hands.

CHAPTER 25
Fish Stories

The boys all helped Dad provide extra meat for the family and managed to have fun and develop some important skills in the process. As soon as the mackerel and other fish began running in Scarborough Bay, Dad and his brother Toy borrowed a boat and took their sons on fishing trips. Earle, Edward, and later, young Leroy piled into the truck with Dad, drove down Beech Ridge Road and collected Toy and his sons Clarence, Leon, and Olaf, and headed for Scarborough Landing and the waiting boat. The boys dug worms the afternoon before and readied their poles and lines. Mama packed extra food for the hungry fishermen.

Out they rowed in their dingy or motor boat. Dad and Toy made good use of these sturdy sons to propel the vessel. They knew to keep very quiet as they settled into a good location and took turns dropping their lines into the water. In hushed voices, Toy and Dad related stories as they waited for the fish to bite.

Toy told stories of their grandfathers in Norway and Sweden, who had fished for their families. No doubt the older brothers added stories about Viking ancestors. One favorite story featured Dad's father, August Ahlquist, and his adventures as he sailed around the world as a young man, then traveled from Sweden to America. August, whom they called Pa, served as a cabin boy in his grandfather's ship when he was only seven years old and had learned to navigate by watching the stars. The stars were points of light that served as guides to direct a seaman to the ship's destination. God had placed the stars in the heavens to act as directional markers, the storyteller said. The idea of using stars to tell direction fascinated the boys, and they determined to ask Pa how ships navigated in more modern times.

These stories quieted the boys until they had a nibble, then another. Pretty soon they had a boat full of fish to bring to Mama. The boys had an exhilarating time hauling in pounds of fish, which sometimes required special skill. Dad and Toy showed the boys how to grasp the jaws of the fish, extract the hook, and make sure it was no longer thrashing about. Once unhooked, the fish were laid in the bottom of the boat on a tarp that was layered with bits of seaweed. Quickly they covered each fish.

The boys learned a trick of baiting the hook with a small piece of torn white undershirt in place of a worm. In fast water the white fabric acted as a lure. To the boys this was amazing, but they knew they were going to have to explain to their mothers why their shirts were torn up! Bringing home supper ought to have some privilege, they reasoned; an occasional torn shirt was a small price to pay for the day's catch.

They arrived home happy but definitely smelling "fishy" as they traipsed into the work kitchen, where Mama and Flonnie had arranged a big 30-gallon oak barrel, pails of water, a pail of rock salt, and a work table with knives on hand. Setting aside the fish that would be eaten fresh that night, they preserved the rest for winter meals.

Working together, they cleaned the fish with the knives, tossing the entrails into a pail to be added to the manure pile. They layered the barrel with salt, fish, and a small amount of water, where it cured for two days or more. In the dead of winter, Mama baked the fish after rolling it in corn meal and topping it with a white sauce "gravy"; or she made a nice fish chowder. Because of the amount of rock salt used, Mama had to soak the fish in fresh water before cooking. It was ever so good, even better when the boys exchanged fish stories at the dinner table.

Simple Fish Chowder

In large bowl cover salted fish to soak for about an hour. This draws out the excess salt.

In kettle melt ½ cup butter over low heat. Add 1 cut-up onion and several stalks of chopped celery. Peel and dice 4-6 potatoes. Add carrots if desired. Add the potatoes and carrots to the onions and a small amount of water just to cover, but no more. Add salt and pepper (to taste). When vegetables are almost done, let simmer over low heat.

Remove as many bones from the fish as possible and carefully skin. Throw bones, skins, and water in manure pile. Lay the refreshed fish over the almost cooked vegetables, breaking the fish up a bit. Add fresh cream and whole milk and heat slowly. Don't let milk boil. Cover. When fish flakes, the chowder is done.

That night, after the fishermen returned, Mama recited this poem at bedtime:

The Winds of Fate
by Ella Wheeler Wilcox

One ship drives east and another drives west
With the self-same winds that blow;
 'Tis the set of the sails
 And not the gales
That tells them the way to go.

Like the winds of the sea are the winds of fate
As we voyage along through life;
 'Tis the set of the soul
 That decides its goal
And not the calm or the strife.

CHAPTER 26
Swimming, Picnics, and Family Fun

Staying in touch with Mama's mother's family meant carefully arranging the farm schedule so that several times in the summer the Ahlquists could visit the Waterboro homestead of the Bensons. Everyone had a job to do before the family set out on the journey: preparing picnic lunches, doing the farm duties earlier than usual, and gathering the family, including Chub, for the lengthy drive. Though Mama's mother, Carrie Catherine Benson, had died young, her parents and younger brothers and sisters were still alive.

Arriving at Deer Pond in Waterboro, the Ahlquist crew played with cousins, went swimming, and visited with family. Though the Nonesuch River flowed near their home in Scarborough, the Ahlquist chil-

Swimming at Deer Pond about 1934—Earle, Edward, Dad, Lee Flonnie

Grammie Benson, 1934

dren learned how to swim at Deer Pond or Little Ossipee, with its nice beach and the family cottage nearby.

Grammie Benson, the matriarch of the family, was a force to be reckoned with during these visits. She was a tall, strong woman with very dark eyes and prominently high cheekbones. The children might have been frightened by the stern old woman had it not been for the presence of cousins nearby and Mama and Dad.

Grammie's grandfather, Joseph Henderson, was of Scottish heritage and her grandmother, called Hannah Young, was a Native American whose Indian name was Anawetok.

Grammie was skilled in her knowledge of herbal remedies, but her skills had not proved enough to save her daughter, Carrie Catherine, from dying from pneumonia. The family believed that the medicine prescribed for Carrie by the local doctors had caused her to have an allergic reaction that led to her untimely death.

Grammie Benson was determined that all the children in the family *must* learn how to swim. Her manner of instruction was simply to toss the children into the water, whether they were ready or wanted to be submerged or not. Fortunately, Mama had warned Dad of her grandmother's unique approach to swim lessons, so Dad stood ready to catch the children and reassure them as they learned to stay afloat. With a twinkle in his eyes, he told them that Grammie Benson wanted to make sure the children could protect themselves in the water and become competent swimmers. She was proud that all the members of her family had learned how to swim—thanks to her, of course.

Elder Grey Meeting House, Chadbourne's Ridge Road, North Waterboro

On the trip home, Mama and Dad told the curious children that Grammie's sternness was a result of her sadness over the loss of her daughter (Mama's mother) at an early age. She felt a strong need to train and protect the children by making them strong.

The children treasured their time with Uncle Tom Thorpe and Aunt Eva, Uncle Leslie Benson, and cousin Olive, who told them about their Chadbourn and Benson cousins. They also saw the remaining farm that Mama had inherited from her grandparents, Joe Ivory and Jayne Chadbourn, off Emery Road near the old Elder Grey Meeting House on Chadbourne's Ridge Road, where Mama had grown up as a child.

They walked the land with Mama and Dad and saw where Mama had been born, where she attended school, and where she went to church as a child. There on the farm they planted pansies at the graves of Mama's parents and grandparents. Mama always insisted on planting her favorite pretty "funny faces," as she called the pansies Dad had grown from seed in the greenhouse.

Earle handles Nell's reins during the summer of 1935. Leroy, Edward, baby Paulie, and Flonnie stand nearby as Dad watches from the hay wagon at left.

CHAPTER 27
The First Haying

Living on a farm with animals to feed meant that haying the fields became a necessary chore. Dad set aside about 10 acres of the 60 acres of Oak Knoll Farm for hay. Alfalfa and clover were generally part of the mix. Sometimes Dad planted winter rye as well. In addition to their own ten acres devoted to hay, the Ahlquists hayed for two neighbors, Harry Libby and Mim Meserve. Mim Meserve's hay was especially thick because he fertilized it with fish refuse.

Dad used horses for the haying. As Earle became more adept at working with the horses, Dad turned more chores over to him, including the haying job. Initially Flonnie helped with the haying, as Earle handled the horses; as Eddie got older, he became a helper, too. Even at a young age, Eddie (three years younger than Earle) and Leroy (five years younger) were good workers. Dad knew the younger boys would develop into fine helpers.

By age five Earle could handle the gentler horses with skill and care. He climbed onto a barrel so that he could reach the harness and slide it over the waiting head of Fritz or Dick. He used a whiffletree to connect the tracers on the harnesses to hook up with the machinery. Then Earle slipped the bit and reins in place as he led Fritz or Dick to connect them to the wagon. Chub, always on hand, lent his encouragement to the endeavor.

Haying was a complex challenge. It was done in several stages, with the first cut usually undertaken in early July, followed by a second harvest by the end of August. Earle had to hook up the horse to the McCormick -Deering mower used to cut the hay. Chub ran alongside as Earle guided Dick down the first row. Methodically Earle moved Dick over the fields as the McCormick sheared the hay to the ground. Acre by acre they went, cutting the hay. Areas near the trees had to be cut by hand with a scythe.

The next stage, a few days later, required a Yankee rake pulled by Dick. This machine rolled hay into piled windrows, tedding the hay as it did this, so that it kicked the hay into the air a bit to air dry it. Everyone prayed for sunny days during this period because the best hay was formed in dry hot weather. It was tiresome work.

Later, everyone went into the field with hay forks to turn the hay by hand to expose it to more drying air. Mama's father, George Chadbourn, had fashioned several of the pitchforks and rakes. A blacksmith like his father before him, he made tools for the neighborhood in Waterboro and Standish. The children felt good about carrying on a tradition, using tools made by a grandfather whom none of them had met since he had died before they were born.

The final hay raking involved a tricky process that required Earle to stand and balance himself by hanging onto Dick's tail so he could reach the raking lever to engage the rake. He was thankful Dick was both patient and well trained.

When the hay had weathered sufficiently, Dad hired a man to bale the hay. After the job was completed, Earle mounted the wagon, with Dick up front and Chub nearby, and headed to the fields to collect the baled hay into the wagon. For large loads, Earle used the team of Dick and Nell.

Sisters and brothers all joined in the task. With pitch forks in hand, they worked together to load the wagon with hay. Once filled, the wagon took the load to the barn, where the hay was stored for winter's feed for the animals.

Mama always had Haymaker's Switchell on hand to refresh their thirst. It was a recipe from Mama's grandmother. This was followed by a swim in the river. The cool water refreshed the young swimmers, and they felt good, knowing that they had helped provide food for the animals that cared for them in turn.

Haymaker's Switchell

1 cup brown sugar

½ teaspoon ginger

½ cup molasses

¾ cup vinegar

2 quarts chilled water

Mix all and keep in stoneware jug.

That evening Mama recited Longfellow's "The Village Blacksmith" when they asked her about her father.

George Chadbourn, Mama's father, was a blacksmith.

CHAPTER 28
The Blacksmith

Mama's family came from Waterboro, Maine. Mama was very close to her grandparents, Joseph Ivory Chadbourn and Jayne Clough Chadbourn, who raised her after her mother died when Mama was only seven. Joseph Ivory Chadbourn and his father, Ivory Chadbourn, had plied the blacksmithing trade along with their other jobs of logging, farming, and sawmilling. Joseph's son George (Mama's father) followed in the family footsteps and became a blacksmith as well. His customers were mostly local farmers and loggers in Waterboro and nearby Standish.

George Chadbourn died soon after Mama and Dad married, so none of the children knew their grandfather. But Mama often thought of him when she recited Longfellow's "The Village Blacksmith" or whenever the children used the handmade tools fashioned by their grandfather, great-grandfather, and great-great-grandfather. She reminded the children that the blacksmithing trade was part of their heritage.

Dad handled those tools with care and instructed his sons in their care, as did Pa. Tools were costly, but these were especially valued because family had made them. Pa told the children a story an old blacksmith had told him. The old blacksmith had said, "There is only one thing that I fear; and that is to be thrown into the scrap heap." He explained. "When I temper steel, I first heat it, hammer it, and then suddenly plunge it into a bucket of cold water. Soon I discover if it will take tempering, or if it will go to pieces in the process. One or two tests will tell me if it will allow itself to be tempered. If not, I toss it into the scrap heap to sell to the junkman when he comes around. It will sell for a cent a pound.

"So I figure when the Lord tests me, too, by fire, water, and hard blows by the heavy hammer; it must be to determine if I will prove fit for the test, or if I will not prove a fit subject for the tempering process. I don't want to be fit only for the scrap heap."

Pa related this story as he instructed the boys how to care for the tools. Dad stood nearby, nodding. Nothing more needed to be said. The boys understood.

CHAPTER 29
Preparing for Christmas

Christmas was always a special holiday for the Ahlquists. The family incorporated many old traditions from Norway and Sweden, which spread the festive occasion over about 30 days, starting on St. Lucia's Day (December 13) and continuing past the New Year, concluding on Twelfth Night, which fell around Epiphany (January 6). The family's celebration of Christmas was actually held on Christmas Eve.

Because the Ahlquists sold Christmas trees, wreaths, and roping, the family began mobilizing for the season about November 1, when trees were harvested, boughs were clipped for the wreath-making, and the summer kitchen became a massive work station. All of this had to be done before Thanksgiving, when stores hung their decorations for Christmas.

Stories of Christmas long ago, the Bethlehem nativity, Nordic Jule fests, and Thanksgiving stories were woven into the busy-ness of the two seasons. By then, Mama and Dad had already made the children's gifts and hidden them in a closet to emerge on Christmas Eve. No one was ever left out, and there were always extra mittens knitted for neighborhood children who had little. Since the children were involved in school pageants, part of the bedtime ritual included practicing the poems to be recited at school.

Pa had developed a Christmas tree business, and several of his sons did similar work to glean extra income around the holidays. Dad rented a stand at Fessenden Park from the city of Portland to sell his trees. He maintained that same location for 30 years, selling Christmas trees to local holiday shoppers.

In 1927 a fierce ice storm struck the region before Christmas. Dad had wisely taken the precaution of covering his trees before the storm. Almost all of the other tree dealers had not anticipated a storm and had done nothing to protect their trees. The ice damaged their trees so severely that they had to discard them. Dad, however, sold all his trees.

Several months earlier Dad had purchased stumpage from a number of landowners. That spring, he made verbal agreements with the landowners to buy their Christmas trees, so the agreement was in place come November when he needed to harvest the trees.

The tree business was a partnership; Dad cut and sold the trees; Mama made wreaths and roping from fir boughs to sell. The Christmas endeavor became a family project when the children became old enough to participate. They learned many valuable lessons from the tree business:

- Identifying a proper woodlot and suitable trees,
- Negotiating an advantageous deal with lot owners,
- Treating both the land and individuals with respect,
- Crafting and displaying the product, and
- Understanding and responding to buyers' needs.

It became Earle's job to gather fir boughs and limbs suitable for the wreaths. He and Chub went to the barn, where he climbed onto a nearby barrel. Earle could then reach over to harness old Fritz and attach him to the express wagon. With Chub next to him in the wagon, Earle headed into the woods with a sharpened hatchet nearby. Six-year-old Earle developed an experienced eye to spot good full, nicely colored boughs. Quickly he cut and tossed them into the back of the wagon, turned the loaded wagon, and headed Fritz back to the farm.

The boughs were unloaded into the summer kitchen, which had become the work room. Flonnie trimmed the boughs and snipped the fir into smaller lengths for Mama to weave into tight wreaths. Mama received eight cents a wreath. On good days she was known to produce 100 wreaths. One buyer from Boston came to the farm to purchase the wreaths he ordered. He tested the wreaths by picking up each one and flinging it across the room against the wall. If it stayed together after hitting the wall, he bought it.

By early December Mama had completed her work of wreath making, giving her time to devote to the traditional baking, cleaning the house, and keeping the children on track and the farm running steadily as Dad still focused on the Christmas tree sales. Mama and her young crew baked an enormous amount of cookies, not only for their own household consumption but also for gift giving and to have available for events at the local school, church or Community Club. Flonnie and the older boys became adept at helping out—from keeping the wood fires burning to stirring pans of batter or just sampling (their favorite chore!).

In between chores, the children listened to stories of holidays from long ago and practiced roles in the upcoming Christmas pageants. When Earle was in the third grade, he was selected to learn a very long poem. Miss Haskell knew his mother would work with him to learn the 131 lines of "Annie & Willie's Prayer" [see Appendix for poems and Christmas recipes]. The year before, Florence had recited "Twas the night before Christmas."

Each evening Mama and Earle worked on the poem together. The evening of the recital, the family filed in, and Earle stood up and recited all of "Annie & Willie's Prayer" without a hitch. The following year when Edward was in the first grade, he dutifully recited "Santa's Cake." Years later, long after each child had forgotten those childhood poems, Mama could recite them on Christmas Eve, much to the family's delight.

Sometimes after dinner when Mama needed to sneak off to tend to work away from the children, Dad told stories from Norway and Sweden at bedtime. Though Dad wasn't born in Norway like his mother was or Sweden like his father, he knew the stories Ma and Pa had told him and he shared them with his children.

Norway was called the Land of the Midnight Sun because in the summer the sun shown day and night, with a gradual time of darkness about midnight. In the wintertime there was almost no daylight and many long hours of murky darkness covered the land. He would laugh and say, "No wonder they became Vikings! They were trying to leave the darkness!" Dad said night time was when trolls were the busiest. They could get away with more mischief in darkness than in light. So to chase away dark spirits in Norway or Sweden, families welcomed the Christ child earlier in the season that those living in other places. A thorough cleaning of the household and the baking of sweet rolls began December 1 so as to be ready for St. Lucia's Day on December 13. Baking began in earnest on St. Lucia's Day. Evergreen boughs filled the house with their beautiful balsam fragrance. Special food was always put out for the animals since everyone believed that animals spoke to God at Christmastime, as the animals came together to celebrate Christ's birth in Bethlehem.

In the early afternoon of Christmas Eve day, the family gathered in the sled, with warm blankets around them. They harnessed old Fritz, the draft horse, and gathered at their grandparent's home for the larger family gathering. They carefully decorated the tree and enjoyed lots of special food. As the Jule tide story was read, they joined hands, sang carols, and danced around the tree. Mama played the piano, Aunt Georgie played the accordion, and Dad played the fiddle and the harmonica as dancers whirled around the dance floor and young children huddled around the edges so as not to get stepped on by flying feet.

It was always wonderful!

CHAPTER 30
Model Ts and Mechanical Marvels

Dad often lost patience with automotive vehicles, though he appreciated the work they did. He didn't much understand the mechanics of them; but, Earle, Edward, Leroy, and the cousins looked on these mechanical pieces with relish. Experimentation (trial and error) provided their education; their tools were a pair of pliers and a monkey wrench. When they got in over their heads with a project, Maynard and Joe Meserve were often ready to lend a helping hand.

The Ahlquists had an automobile—a truck or a coupe—early on. For Dad, though, nothing ever really replaced the horses. After all, as Dad said, a person could talk to a horse. Because of the condition of the roads and the early design of the tires, cars tended to be seasonal vehicles, used from spring to fall. Usually the family car would be put up on blocks in the barn for the winter in order to preserve the tires. Not one to let a good motor sit idle, Dad attached a belt to the tire axle, which was attached to a saw blade, enabling the engine to double as a wood cutter. During good weather, when the roads were clear, the family car or truck filled its primary use as a means of transportation.

Once a year Howard Carter came to the farm to charge the batteries for the cars and trucks. He carried a large charging coil, which was connected to a big battery. Model T Fords that were driven in colder climates and put up for the winter required a yearly charging.

The Ford's foot pedals controlled two forward gears and one reverse; a fourth pedal operated the brake. The spark and throttle were controlled by a hand lever on the steering column. A 10-gallon fuel tank was located under the front seat. One of the peculiarities of the early Fords made it necessary for drivers to put the car in reverse and steer it up steep hills backward. This was because gasoline was fed to the engine by gravity, and the reverse gear had more power than the forward gears. Mama became quite adept at managing the reverse trek up hills.

The most direct route from the Ahlquist farm to Sherman's store in North Scarborough, required driving over challenging terrain on Beech Ridge Road. From Sherman's Store the car then traveled on to Westbrook to the library or on to Gorham. Hills marked the route either way. Oak Knoll Farm stood on the crest of a hill. Due west was the Meserve Farm and the old Marr Farm at the top of the hill. Down the long hill, Beech Ridge Road crossed the Nonesuch River. Beyond the river's bridge another Meserve farm lay to the left, nestled in a small valley. Beech Ridge Road traveled to the top of Sand Hill and from there followed straight, flat terrain to Sherman's Store and the Grange Hall.

The trickiest part of the journey was negotiating Sand Hill. As the name suggests, that section of the road—even after some early paving—remained quite sandy. The narrow tires on the early Fords made the trek more difficult. As the car angled upward on the prolonged incline, the rear main bearing began losing oil. To prevent that from happening, Mama had to stop at the Meserves, turn the car around, and back up Sand Hill, trying to avoid the sandy spots that threatened to mire the car. At that point, Mama enlisted the children's help. Little ones scooched down in their seats so as not to block the view, and Flonnie and Earle served as lookouts, keeping a sharp eye out for ruts and sandy spots and alerting their mother so she could avoid them. Once at the top, she turned the car around in the Lord's driveway, at the crest of the hill, and proceeded forward to the desired destination. No wonder Dad preferred horses!

When a car broke down, Dad hitched up old Fritz or Dick, hooked a chain onto the faulty car, and hauled the "broken" car into the field. Dad then bought a replacement if he could find a used one at a good price. That gave the brothers plenty of opportunity to practice their skill in auto mechanics and repair. They took the old car apart and tried to get it running again. Their "repair shop" consisted of an old mattress, which they placed on the lawn and on which they lay while working on the defective car. Dick provided the "horse power." The horse pulled the broken car to the lawn, settled it near the mattress, and tipped it on its side so the boys could work on the engine underneath.

The Ford engines were fairly simple and efficient with all four cylinders cast into a single block. The cylinder head was detachable for easy access and repair. The engine generated 20 horsepower and attained a speed of 40-45 miles per hour. The engine was mounted with three pivot points. Tools to fix these mechanical wonders were rather scarce, so the boys treated the tools they had with care. The Ahlquist boys were more fortunate than many because they had tools that had been made by their blacksmith grandfather; though they had to admit, Grampa Chadbourn's blacksmith tools were more suitable for horses than cars. But they made do. Grampa George Chadbourn had owned a 1906 Buick, and though he never drove himself, he had hired a driver to take him places in it.

By 1937 Mama decided Flonnie, at age 13, needed to learn to drive so she could help with the milk deliveries to Riverton Dairy. Earle, 11, had already taught himself to drive, so Mama enlisted his help to teach Flonnie the intricacies of mastering the Ford. The lessons focused on how to work the pedals and the spark and throttle levers in proper order—a complicated sequence that had to be exact or the car wouldn't go. Mama trusted Earle to guide his sister through the process.

Flonnie, determined to learn, concentrated on Earle's methodical instructions. During the adventure, she mowed down a hay rack when she failed to turn and brake in time, but fortunately no one was injured. Under Earle's expert tutelage, Flonnie learned to drive and qualified for her driver's license. At 13 she had already entered high school (having skipped several grades), looked older than her years, and stood 5'8" tall. Like the boys, Flonnie became quite proficient in quick repairs that might be required. Baling wire and a few basic tools could do wonders!

In 1938 Dad bought a Farmall 812 tractor to ease the workload on the family and the old horses. Thinking he had mastered the mechanics of running the tractor, he was showing Earle how to drive it along a newly planted row, when much to his surprise, he found himself driving right over the new rows—destroying them in the process. All Dad could do was say, "Whoa, whoa!" It was obvious Dad still remained much more at ease with horses. Nevertheless, he continued in his efforts to modern-

Earle, 15, helped Ira Dresser move this Federal-style house in 1941.

ize the farm, for Mama's sake and to keep in step with a world that was becoming more automated.

As a teenager, Earle had a Ford coupe that Mama named Nasturtium because of the paint job Earle had bestowed on it—a greenish yellow with shades of orange. The going fare for a pretty girl who wanted a ride in the two-seater was a well-written book report.

In the summer of 1941, when Earle was 15, Ira Dresser hired him to help move a large Federal-style building on outer Congress Street in Portland. Space was needed for an airport, and the large home was to be moved about 500 yards across Congress Street and up a rise. The path crossed a major highway, and the house had to be carefully situated on a knoll. Earle drove a chain-driven Sterling truck, gas-fueled, with six wheels and a one-inch cable to handle the job, which took about six weeks. This was Earle's first experience with such a massive building moving project and with such a large, high-powered truck.

As head of a three-man crew, Earle received instructions from Ira Dresser, who checked in daily. The first step involved cutting and trimming solid hardwood trees to be used as skid beams to transport the large

The Sterling truck Earle used to move a Congress Street house.

building safely through the field and over the road. While this was being done on one side of Congress Street, workers completed the foundation on the knoll where the home would be located. Earle's crew used screw-jacks to encircle the building and secure it on the skid beams. Once this was done, they proceeded slowly and deliberately to pull the large framed building forward with the mighty Sterling truck. Its power was impressive, and Earle came away from the job with a far greater understanding of the power of machinery.

CHAPTER 31
Leading Up to War

The year 1939 opened with hope regarding family finances but worry about world events. On the national scene America was starting to pull out of the economic depression that had such a stranglehold on many cities and towns. The Ahlquists had managed to work through those hard times, and the Beech Ridge community had seen significant improvements.

Mama's health was mending. During her last time in the hospital, she had lost all her beautiful auburn hair, but she was home now, gaining strength and her hair was growing back—though coming in white. Mama and Dad made a practice of moving forward and counting their blessings daily. They lived on a paved road and enjoyed electricity and the handy appliances it powered, the greenhouse was doing well, the livestock was healthy, and everyone was gaining health. The family was making significant headway in paying off their hospital bills and cheerfully meeting their obligation. A week's groceries could be purchased at Sherman's store for $10 with change to spare, and gas remained cheap. Florence, now 14, and Earle, 12, both held part-time jobs in addition to the usual farm and school work. Their earnings helped boost the family's finances, and the jobs proved to be fine learning opportunities for the two. Edward, 9, and Leroy, 7, picked up the slack around the farm by tending to the animals and bringing in wood for the wood stove. Little Paulie, 3, thought the sun rose and set on big sister Florence as she tried to emulate her in every way.

Not all was rosy, however. The radio brought disturbing news from Europe of Adolph Hitler's systematic takeover of adjacent countries. Germany annexed Austria in 1938. Ma and Pa were especially concerned about family in Norway, fearful about the spreading unrest in Europe. Church friends shared news of worrisome events in northern Europe. From his sailor friends Pa heard of unsettling news from Canada, Scotland, and Great Britain. Pa read newspapers from several European countries and tried to balance out fact from fiction. Dad watched the economic trends, knowing that when the price of certain goods rose, it indicated a growing demand for those items. Earle overheard Pa and Dad discussing the increase in the price of metal. Pa and Dad recalled how leather spiked upward before the Great War, indicating the need for more leather goods to harness cavalry. Though adults were watchful, they did not openly discuss the situation or their fears.

Twelfth night had only just passed and the family was preparing to celebrate Paulie's fourth birthday when Dad applied to work at a sheet metal yard, called the Plate Yard, in nearby South Portland. Rumors began to circulate that the area's metal shops might expand to meet the need for metal for new ships for Great Britain and possibly France as those countries prepared to resist Germany's escalating aggression. President Roosevelt, the rumor mill advised, might be considering ramping up aid for America's European allies. Hearing this, Pa and Dad foresaw the need for increased steel construction on the local front.

Despite the turmoil abroad, the family celebrated Paulie's fourth birthday in January with gusto. The meal that day *had* to include Mama's home-cut French fries. Mama had introduced them to the family's menu fairly recently, and Paulie loved them. The little girl didn't care what else was on the menu as long as she had French fries and pink cake for dessert. For the main meal, Mama prepared a meat roll with gravy and carrots. She baked Paulie's favorite Very Good Cake with care, topping it with raspberry preserves and whipped cream to fulfill Paulie's wish for a pink cake.

The birthday girl greased and floured the baking pan as Mama and Flonnie mixed the cake batter. Edward and Leroy had the assignment of keeping the wood stove's oven at a moderate temperature with just the right wood to maintain the heat. Mama and Flonnie took turns beating the batter vigorously as the recipe required.

Very Good Cake:

In a big mixing bowl put:
2 cups of sugar
2 cups of flour (mixed together with a fork)
6 eggs
½ pound soft butter
2 teaspoons vanilla flavoring

Beat vigorously for a full 15 minutes, turn into a prepared pan, and bake for 45-60 minutes, depending on the size of the pan. Cool and apply icing.

Once the cake was done, Mama put it on the back pantry shelf to cool while she and Flonnie whipped a cup of cream and folded in about three tablespoons of Mama's raspberry jam. They lathered this delicious pink stuff on the cooled cake. Yummy!

Dad celebrated the next birthday, in March. By then he had already figured out how much seed to plant and looked longingly at the land, anxious to work it. Watching Dad pour over seed catalogs, Earle shook his head and asked, "Gardens are a lot of work, Dad. Why do you expand it almost every year?"

"Earle, this little seed holds the gift of possibilities," Dad replied. "I never look at it for what it is now, but rather, what it will become."

Smiling, Mama rubbed Dad's shoulder and said, "Earle, we always need to nurture the possibilities in these seeds or this old world would just become a briar patch. Besides, I know you enjoy the results."

Dad added, "Much of what those Liberty ships are carrying is food-stuffs. America is feeding free Europe."

Raising food, Earle realized, was one way his parents could take action for good; they were doing what they could, wherever they could.

Winter had dragged on, especially as Americans continued to hear foreboding news from Europe. Earlier in the month Germany had swallowed up Czechoslovakia. But determined to stay on a positive note, Dad and Mama kept the family busy with the usual farm duties and extra work that could be undertaken to supplement the farm's coffers.

By April spring had finally come, and the family looked forward to Leroy's eighth birthday. They happily began the planting, using the greenhouse to an advantage, and cared for rabbits, chickens, horses, and cows. Flonnie was doing well in high school, and endured with good humor Dad's frequent reminders to "Stand tall!" Earle had graduated from Beech Ridge Community School and was attending seventh grade classes at rooms temporarily set up in the high school until the new Oak Hill School was completed. Consequently, Earle and Flonnie headed out of the house by 6 A.M to arrive at school on time. It was a long walk or run, if they got a late start.

In many ways the larger world began opening up for Flonnie and Earle. For the first time they shared classes with pupils from other parts of Scarborough; their new school was not limited to students from their close-knit Beech Ridge community. Edward and Leroy still attended Beech Ridge Community School, where Aunt Ruth was their teacher.

In May Earle celebrated his birthday. As the weather warmed, the Ahlquist children carefully tended the sprouting vegetables recently transplanted from the greenhouse. Spring signaled the arrival of wild strawberries that could be added to the homemade ice cream Earle savored as a special birthday treat. If the hens were laying well, Mama made a maple walnut angel food cake, a great accompaniment to the strawberry ice cream; otherwise she prepared a butternut cake with maple frosting. Either way, Mama made it special. She did that for all the children on their birthdays.

Spring marked the end of the cold season and the necessity of taking a spoonful of cod liver oil every night before bedtime. Family members were plagued by coughs less frequently in the spring, which lessened the need to keep kerosene and sugar heating on the back of the stove as a remedy. There were many things to celebrate in spring! It did not seem to matter that chaos reigned in Europe; so far, the Ahlquist cousins in Norway remained safe, and the big ocean between America and Italy and Germany served to insulate the family from the threatening war clouds over Europe. But Earle and Flonnie noticed that Pa and Dad listened to the news more attentively and remained watchful.

That summer Flonnie worked in the early mornings at George Rogers's bakery business. Earle joined her at the firm in the spring of 1941. The siblings found George Rogers to be a good man and kind. A Greek immigrant who had taken the name George Rogers, he had a clear sense of fairness and the value of work. Rogers' Bakery, located on the corner of Sewall and Congress Streets in Portland, supplied many restaurants and stores in the area with bread, rolls, and pies. All of them tasted homemade. Flonnie proved proficient in handling the pie crusts. Earle worked as a general helper and delivery man. After his first week of work, Earle joined the other workers, who were lined up to collect their pay in cash. They had been hired to work for $1 a day. As Mr. Rogers came through the line, paying each boy, he pulled Earle aside, indicating he wanted to speak to him alone.

Earle feared he had lost his job. But when Mr. Rogers returned, he gave Earle $2 a day, saying, "This is between you and me, because you earned it and I am glad to give it to you."

That extra money made a huge difference for the family. George Rogers proved to be an exceptional employer for the Ahlquist siblings. He paid them a fair wage, not merely according to the number of hours they worked but also according to how hard and carefully they performed. In addition, he allowed them to use his truck to attend the Saturday confirmation classes held at First Lutheran Church on Elm Street in Portland. And he paid them for a full day even though part of that time was spent in church. Mr. Rogers was always true to his word and believed in encouraging good children.

Earle got his driver's license with Mr. Rogers's help. He used the Rogers delivery truck to test for his license. The delivery truck had only one seat—for the driver. Passengers had to sit on a wooden delivery box tipped on its side---not a cushiony seat, by any means. Commercial Street, where the driving test took place, was paved with cobblestones and was crisscrossed with tracks that accommodated the trolley cars that ran along the route. This was a bumpy ride at the very least.

On the day of the test, Earle drove to the Motor Vehicle Bureau in the delivery truck. The officer assigned to test the young driver climbed into the truck and perched himself on the makeshift seat as Earle started the engine and began to drive the instructed route.

It seemed to Earle that he had driven only a block or so when the officer abruptly said, "I see you can drive quite well. Consider you have passed."

Surprised, Earle said, "Shall I turn around and bring you back to the station?"

"No. No," the officer said. "I can get out right here and walk. I'll meet you there." The officer hurried out of the truck and headed for the MVB office, while Earle reversed his route.

At the end of August 1939, Edward turned 10 and began assuming more responsibilities around the farm. He was particularly good with the gardening and caring for the cows. Often, when Earle and Edward milked the cows early in the morning, they noticed that Leroy used only one hand because the other hand was holding a book. The older boys rolled their eyes and vowed to make him pay for his inattention later.

In September the radio broadcast the news that Germany had invaded Poland, an ally of France and Great Britain. This act of aggression marked the beginning of World War II in Europe. On September 3, 1939, Britain and France declared war on Germany. Once Great Britain entered the European war, Pa and Dad knew that America would soon become part of the supply chain to produce food and other needed goods for the Allies. Within weeks, activity at the South Portland Navy Yard increased, and rumors spread that the yard would be building ships for Great Britain.

Back at the Ahlquist farm, life continued as before, with the haying and the harvest, Beech Ridge Community Club gatherings, church on Sundays, and caring for each other as well as gearing up for the usual Christmas tree season. Mama continued to gain in strength and was able to work longer, though Dad still relied on Flonnie for many household chores so as not to overburden Mama. Dad was pleased that Earle, Eddie, and Leroy were taking on more of the farm's responsibilities, especially with the possibility that there might be work for Dad at the shipyard.

When school reopened in January 1940 after the Christmas break, Earle and his classmates had to carry their books and other supplies and walk in single file to the newly opened Oak Hill School, about a mile away. They would be the first class to graduate from Oak Hill School that June. On graduation day, Earle was the first student to march across the stage to receive his eighth-grade diploma. A few days later, Flonnie received her high school diploma, five days before her 16th birthday. She was the youngest student in her class, having skipped two grades. The whole family proudly celebrated graduation day for the two siblings and the many Ahlquist cousins who also received their diplomas that June.

Mama made Flonnie a new dress for the occasion and arranged a festive graduation party at the farm, complete with ice cream and an assortment of tasty treats. A particular favorite was strawberry ice cream, and Mama made sure there was plenty on hand. Edward, Leroy, and Paulie helped with the preparations. The hand-cranked ice cream maker was stored in the ice house to keep it chilled for optimum use. The bucket was packed one-third full with crushed ice alternating with rock salt. Then the inner cylinder was loaded with ice cream ingredients.

Homemade Ice Cream:

Beat 6 egg yolks.
Combine with 2 cups milk, 1 cup sugar, and dash of salt in the top of a double boiler.
Cook until mixture resembles a thick custard, then cool.
When sufficiently cool, pour mixture into the ice cream cylinder.
Add: 4 cups heavy cream
2 cups crushed strawberries
a squeeze of lemon
Churn until the desired consistency.
Makes 2 full quarts of ice cream.
Simpler recipes did not use egg yolks or require cooking a custard.

Once the ingredients were in the cylinder, the hard work of cranking the ice cream machine began. Everyone took turns with the crank until the ice cream reached just the right consistency. Occasionally the person operating the crank stopped and added more ice. After the churning had ceased, the children had to wait while the ice cream was packed with ice to keep it hard until dessert time. The waiting became a bit easier, though, when Mama pulled out the dasher (the plunger that churned the ice cream), and everyone scraped off spoonfuls of the world's best frozen dessert.

Feeling the need to spread her wings a bit, yet somewhat limited by age and the fact that she was a young woman, Flonnie considered what she would do next. Mama encouraged her to search for appropriate work. Flonnie first worked for a family in Portland who needed child care because the mother was ill. Having taken care of several younger siblings, Flonnie knew she had the skills for the job. However, she soon discovered that the children were quite undisciplined and the parents did not support her efforts to enforce discipline. Neighbor Hazel Merry came to Flonnie's rescue. Hazel hired Flonnie and her cousin Frances to tend her diner, which was located off Commercial Street near Rufus Deering Lumberyard. It proved to be a very busy spot for breakfast and lunch. Flonnie moved in with Hazel, and she and Frances ran the diner.

Flonnie, at 16, became so proficient at running the diner that she soon became its proprietor. She rose every morning at 2:30 A.M. and baked the bread, doughnuts, and rolls for the 6 A.M. customers. After a mid-morning lull, luncheon patrons filled the diner. By mid-afternoon the diner closed, and Flonnie had free time to rest, visit friends, and shop. Unfortunately, no one warned the young business owner about frozen pipes in the winter. When the pipes burst, Flonnie closed the diner and sought other work.

Dad and Mama assured her that even catastrophes provided a learning experience, and there was no loss unless she did not learn. Flonnie agreed it was certainly a learning experience, but the fact that Dad had to bail her out of the situation by clearing her debt of $60 upset her. Mama and Dad encouraged her to take time to evaluate the good and bad of the experience. She was grateful for the guidance and took it to heart.

After the diner fiasco, Flonnie worked for Dad selling Christmas trees and with Mr. Rogers at his bakery. Flonnie also did bookkeeping work for Otis Lilly, who ran a garage in Scarborough. Flonnie constantly looked for opportunities to gain work experience and contribute her skills in a meaningful way.

Meanwhile, the shadow of war overseas continued to hang over the Ahlquist family and the world. On April 9, 1940, Germany invaded

Denmark and Norway and occupied the homeland of the family's many cousins still living in that region. On May 10 Germany invaded Belgium, the Netherlands, and Luxemburg. A week later, on May 17, Germany invaded France. On June 14, just a few days after Flonnie's graduation, Germany occupied Paris, and France surrendered eight days later.

CHAPTER 32
The Day Which Would Live in Infamy

Sunday, December 7, 1941, began as a regular day at the Ahlquist farm, with the usual farm chores and animal tending. After that was done, Flonnie, Edward, and Leroy accompanied Dad to tend the Christmas tree stand with Dad. Armed with thermoses of coffee and warm milk, cookies, and sandwiches, they piled into the truck to travel to Portland, while Earle, Paulie, and Mama tended to business at home.

Mama had delivered wreaths and swags to Boston and Portland stores for their holiday decorations, and she was catching up with the socks that needed darning. Earle kept the fire burning and churned the butter. Mama said she preferred Earle or Edward to help with the butter churning because Flonnie and Leroy always seemed to be holding a book with one hand while handling the churn with the other. Though she approved of their love of reading, she wondered if it did not shortchange the butter a bit. She settled into her rocking chair with her basket of darning next to her, while Paulie played with paper dolls on the floor. Mama asked Earle to turn the radio up a bit, to compensate for the sound of the noisy butter paddle. She wanted to hear the carols on the radio, a welcome sound that contributed to her Christmas spirit.

After increasing the volume on the radio, Earle poured the heavy cream into the wooden butter churn, inserted the churn paddle, attached the cover, and started turning the churner crank until he heard the sound of splashing milk. Nearby on the table he had readied a large butter bowl, a long-handled wooden spoon, the butter molds, a pitcher of chilled water, and salt. The bread was rising in the loaf pans, and his mouth began to water as he thought of the fresh butter on the hot bread—a tasty reward for his hard work.

The serene musical strains of "Oh Little Town of Bethlehem" stopped abruptly, and a reporter's intense voice interrupted the programming with a special announcement. Earle stopped the churn and turned up the radio. Mama stopped her rocking. In somber tones, the reporter informed the American people that Japanese planes and ships had attacked the U.S. Naval Base at Pearl Harbor on the Pacific island of Hawaii, killing many American sailors and sinking and damaging naval ships.

The color drained from Mama's cheeks. Even Paulie stopped her humming and sat still.

The following day, President Franklin Delano Roosevelt would describe December 7 as "a date which will live in infamy. . . ."

With a trembling but clear voice, Mama turned to Earle and said, "They'll be coming for you to fight, Earle."

"They won't have to come for me, Mama. I will go willingly," Earle replied. Mama knew her son well enough to know it was true; but there was time yet, he was only fifteen.

The radio announcer continued with a few more details, then the Christmas carols continued. Six-year-old Paulie had stopped her play and looked back and forth at her mother and her brother. Mama patted her hand, then gently started rocking again as Earle continued sloshing the churn. Paulie blinked her big blue eyes and silently went back to playing with her dolls as the sound of carols wafted through the room.

Mama and Earle both knew that they must go on with the work at hand, systematically putting one foot in front of the other, performing the duty at hand—the same way the family had faced each challenge—doing the next thing, while very aware that the horizon had changed dramatically.

They waited for Dad, Flonnie, Edward, and Leroy to return home that evening—and they worked as they waited. They knew what the discussion would be focused on at the table that evening. But they also knew they were together, they still had blessings to count, and there was work at hand to do.

Homemade Butter:

1 quart heavy cream
½ teaspoon salt
Chilled water

Pour cream into the butter churn. Put on cover and insert wooden churner. Mash churner up and down until butter sounds like splashing milk. Take out butter with spoon, leaving milk in churn. Put butter in butter bowl adding water and work with paddles. Pour milky water back into churn. Continue until clean water only, adding small amount of salt and work in with paddles. When the desired consistency has been reached, remove the butter, set in molds, and leave in cool place to set.

Take remaining butter and spread on hot bread. Enjoy!

Throw milky water into pigpens.

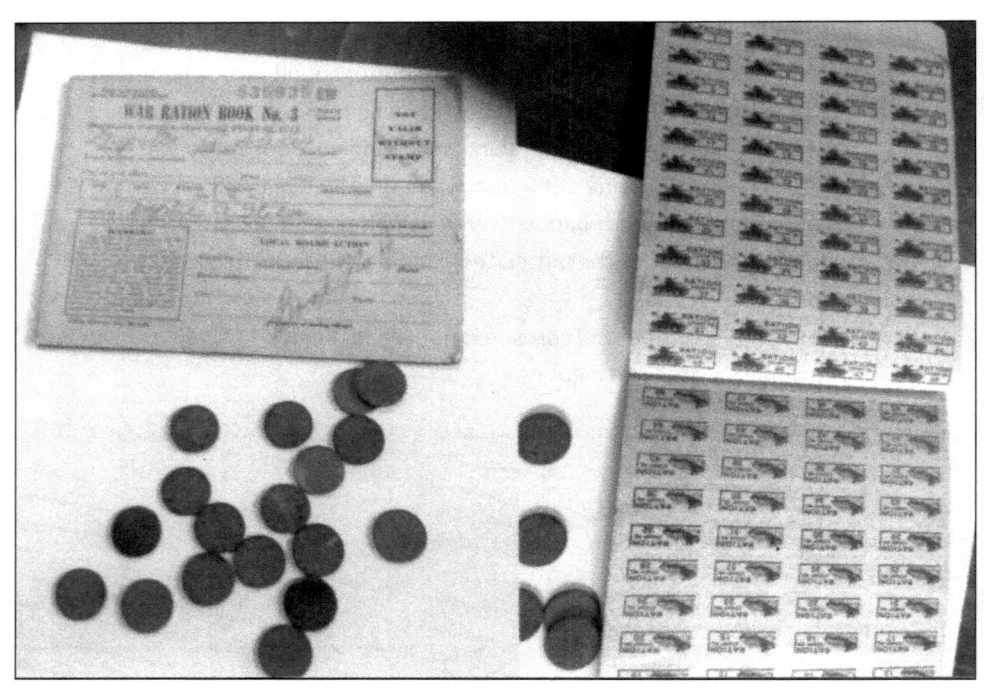

Coupon ration books from World War II.

CHAPTER 33
Pearl Harbor and Its Aftermath

When Dad, Flonnie, Edward, and Leroy headed off for the Christmas tree stand in Portland, they were anticipating brisk sales. December 7, 1941, seemed like a propitious day in many respects. City Hall was featuring a concert of Handel's "Messiah," and Dad hoped the crowd would be in the mood to buy their trees either before or after the concert. The newspapers reported tension with Japan, but it was considered nothing more than "tension." Then suddenly at about 2 P.M., a siren blared from Portland's fire station, and the crowds learned that Pearl Harbor had been bombed.

Dad came home that evening with a special edition of the *Portland Evening Express* announcing the event. The U.S. Navy had notified local customs officials not to allow any foreign ships to sail from port. And a bulletin had gone out that local shipyards and plants working on defense contracts would add extra guards. The Air Raid Service ordered 37 wardens to be stationed at the South Portland Shipyard, where Dad and Toy had been working with others to manufacture cargo ships (dubbed Liberty ships) to aid Great Britain.

When Dad joined the rest of the family gathered around the table for their evening meal, he knew everyone would be discussing the attack. He knew, too, that he and Mama had to set the tone for a practical, honest approach to the news—not panicky, not giving in to fear, but confronting the disastrous event with honesty even in the face of sadness, ready to deal with the pending challenges and aware of the sacrifices they might be called upon to meet. The family's usual grace included an affirmation that this event was no surprise to God, and that He would see them through it. Their faith gave family members confidence that

God understood it all and would guide them in whatever they needed to do, whenever He needed them to do it. Leaving their worries in God's hands, they got on with life and their evening meal, topping their potatoes with Mama's homemade gravy and listening to Dad's report on the shipyard's projects. The first two Liberty ships were due to be launched December 20. He reflected how farmers, loggers, and common laborers had become skilled shipbuilders during the past year. He was proud that Ahlquists were part of the team working to address this need.

Dad, his brother Toy, and his brother-in-law Sigurd Simonsen were working at the yard, and soon his niece Frances and daughter Florence would join the wartime workforce. Other family members engaged in the war effort included Mama's cousins from Waterboro, who were employed at the shipyard; cousin Everett Scribner, who drove the bus transporting workers from Waterboro to the shipyard; and brother-in-law Peter Johnson and brothers Norris and Guy Chadbourn, who were active in coastal defense.

The shipyard workers used an innovative design to mass produce the ships. This was the first time a standardized design using an all-welded construction had ever been implemented. It was a brand new type of ship construction using a sequence of welds and locked-in stresses. The ship's large hull and other subsections were built simultaneously, then joined together. Shipyards began applying Henry Ford's assembly-style production methods to build these cargo ships because of the need to supply the Allies with a large number of ships as quickly as possible. Some were skeptical about using the process for ships, but by the end of the war, 18 U.S. shipyards, including the South Portland plant, would build 2,710 Liberty ships following the same design. Dad and Pa fervently hoped this would mean a shortened war, but that now seemed unrealistic based on the reports they were hearing from Europe and now facing the challenge from Japan. Nevertheless, they determinedly focused on doing what they could, where they could.

It was no surprise when President Franklin D. Roosevelt announced on Monday, December 8, 1941, that the United Stated had declared war on Japan; three days later America declared war on Japan's ally, Germany, and joined the Allies in the hostilities marking World War II.

Months before the Pearl Harbor attack, it was evident to Dad that Casco Bay was becoming a hub of naval activity. According to Peter Johnson and Norris Chadbourn, a terse government announcement on September 16 ordered American naval ships to act as escort convoys to protect British ships carrying vital goods back to Great Britain. The U.S. fleet was ordered to retaliate if attacked by German ships trying to intercept the convoy. With its food imports disrupted, Great Britain looked to American farmers to supplement its stock of meat and produce. Scores of vessels, ranging from patrol craft to battleships, could be seen from Casco Bay. By December 8 harbor defense became more apparent as every sector became affected by the war effort.

At the Ahlquist farm the adjustments were taken in stride as Dad headed off to work at the South Portland shipyard. Flonnie and Frances put in their applications to work there as well, and as soon as they were hired, they rode to work with Uncle Toy, who shared the same work shift. Earle, Edward, and Leroy kept the farm work under control, and Paulie learned housekeeping skills from Mama. Each weekday, Earle, Edward, Leroy, and Paulie headed to school.

All was not work and worry. The young people looked forward to neighborhood dances on Saturday nights at the Broadturn Dance Hall. Dad's good friend, Sam Scott, was usually the caller for the dances. Entrance fee was $1. Florence, Earle, Clarence, Frances, Karine, Althea, and Leon were among the regulars. The music was a welcome relief for the young people. Waltzes, foxtrots, square dances, and quadrilles were always offered, along with a new dance called the jitterbug. Pa Applebee oversaw the dance hall. He lived on the corner of the Burnham Road and the Watson Mill Road in North Saco. Knowing adults like Sam Scott and Mr. Applebee were in attendance, Dad and Mama felt confident this was a safe space for their offspring's recreation. Younger siblings and cousins looked forward to the time they could join the older teens at the dance hall. There were other dance halls in the area, but this was the one approved by Dad and Mama.

During high school Earle made a name for himself in sports; his brothers and cousins would follow suit. With their farm duties, they did not have a lot of extra time for a sports schedule, but when they did play, they performed with distinction. Walking to school and tackling strenuous farm duties produced endurance and strength. Earle set records in track and field and cross-country. He was the first to admit that he often played basketball like a bull; he left the finesse to his younger brother Edward, who distinguished himself on the basketball court. Earle set state records in foot races, discus and javelin throwing, and shot-put. It would be many years before some of those records would be broken in the state of Maine. One day, while walking near Sherman's Store, Earle encountered Morris Cohen, a star runner who had held the record before Earle topped it. Morris gave Earle a hearty congratulations and praised him for "doing Scarborough proud," an act of generosity that Earle remembered with pleasure long afterward.

Other changes emerged in Scarborough as Americans geared up to defeat the enemy. Ration coupon books were issued as more supplies had to be diverted to the troops. Edmund Muskie, a lawyer who would later serve as the state's first Democratic governor in more than 100 years and go on to be U.S. Secretary of State, handled the distribution of ration books at his office beyond Cash Corner in South Portland. People traded coupons to help supply those with special needs. The Beech Ridge Community Club was active as always in this endeavor. Ma often tried to obtain a few more coupons for coffee, which she sent to family overseas. She regularly packed clothing and food, carefully wrapped in layers of newspapers, for passage to their European kin.

Mrs. Frances Libbey, Scarborough High school teacher, asked for Earle's help in the spring of 1942. Leaders in Washington were encouraging people to grow their own produce in "Victory Gardens," and she wanted one. She asked Earle to gather a few strong students and come to her home in the Winnock's Neck area of Scarborough to plow up her front lawn and plant a victory garden as an example to others that this was the "right" thing to do. Earle promptly did just that.

War bonds were sold for $18.75 each at public buildings, post offices, schools, and community gatherings like dances. Competitions were regularly set at the schools with classes vying for first place to see how many war bonds the students could sell.

Local citizens became air raid volunteers and took turns monitoring coastal neighborhoods to make sure lights were out at night. The Casco Bay area was closely monitored to protect the ship building work in nearby South Portland. German submarines were often reported to be close by. A lookout tower, adapted from an ice-fishing hut, was mounted on top of Scarborough High School. Earle was part of the team that moved it into place. They wrapped the hut with strong ropes, slipped a chain and a rope underneath, and pulled the rope over the roof and down the opposite side, as the husky men and boys hoisted the hut onto the school's roof. It was then outfitted with a small wood stove to keep it warm for volunteers who served during the winter months.

So many local people worked at the shipyard, where shipbuilding went on seven days a week, twenty-four hours a day in three shifts, that the town had to hire older men and younger boys to help maintain the roads. Edward was hired for brush cutting at 80 cents an hour, but Leroy was considered too small for the task, much to his disappointment.

As gasoline and tires came under the rationing mandate, people had to make hard decisions. Earle put up his Buick because of the gasoline crunch. Uncle Toy needed replacement tires, so Earle sold the Buick's tires to his uncle for $65 per tire, so rare were the tires.

Innovation became the name of the game as citizens focused on how to adapt. When water in the truck's gas line froze, Uncle Dick told Earle to wrap a cotton clothesline rope around the gas tank to the carburetor and ignite it. Earle followed the directions but stood back hesitantly after lighting the rope. After a few minutes Uncle Dick pulled the rope out; the ice in the line had melted and the truck's engine started.

Parts were hard to find, and when the car's clutch began slipping, Earle used Mama's supply of fuller's earth (clay material used in cleaning and cosmetics) to solve the problem. He dusted the clutch with the material to create traction on the hesitating clutch line. The clutch engaged, and Earle added another item to the family's growing list of adaptations. This spirit of inventiveness proved very helpful throughout the war years. The family learned to make the most of what they had at hand.

Flonnie started working at the South Portland Shipyard in early 1942. When her preliminary test results showed she had an unusual acuity to read and translate graphs, Flonnie was assigned to read the intricate blueprints for producing the ships at the yard. She came home and reported it all to Mama, who just smiled and said, "I just knew when you learned Norwegian knitting from a book and easily mastered those intricate graphs, it would come in use someday. But I never really expected this!"

They both laughed.

Once she was trained to read and interpret the blueprints, Flonnie scrambled from one work area to another to check that the welders followed the plans accurately. Only after Flonnie approved the work did the cranes lift the bow section and transport it to sit on the keel. The operation relied on her keen eye and accurate reading of the blueprints.

CHAPTER 34
Dateline

Each date leading to World War II and America's involvement in it held more significance than the last—for the world and for the members of the Ahlquist family.

September 1940—Congress passes the Selective Service Act in anticipation of entering a war, even though at that time the nation's official policy is one of neutrality. President Roosevelt maintains that an all-volunteer army will not be adequate to fight a war on two fronts. This is the first peacetime draft in U.S. history and requires all men between the ages of 21 and 35 to register. More than 16 million men respond during 1940, and a lottery selects those who will serve. Only about 18,000 are inducted in this first wave, but the number increases to more than 920,000 by 1941 and more than 10 million by the end of World War II.

December 29, 1940—During his "fireside chat" broadcast over the nation's radios, President Roosevelt asserts that even though America is not formally at war, the nation has an obligation to supply its allies with weapons and prepare for its own defense. "We must be the great arsenal of democracy," he tells his fellow citizens.

March 11, 1941—President Roosevelt signs the Land-Lease Act. In order to maintain an official policy of neutrality, the United States can not provide direct aid to its allies; the Land-Lease Act allows America to lend or lease supplies and equipment to Britain and other countries vital to America's national security. In addition to aiding Allied nations, the Act improves the American economy by creating jobs in factories across the nation.

Dec. 7, 1941—Japanese war planes attack Pearl Harbor.

Dec. 8, Dec. 11, 1941—America declares war on Japan and Germany.

June 1942—Flonnie joins the workforce of the South Portland Shipyard. She is trained to read blueprints and becomes a tack welder, then overseer of her division, ascertaining that the steel plates match the blueprints exactly. She is one of the few women selected for this intricate work as a shipfitter.

April 18, 1944—Earle enlists in the U.S. Marine Corp. He is 17 and halfway through his junior year in high school. All of his male classmates except Brenton Dodge (who was joining the ministry) and Stanley Pooler (who was only 16) enlist at the same time. They plan to complete their education when they return, believing that now is the time to step forward and serve America's campaign to win the war.

May 9, 1944—Earle turns 18 and the family holds a party to celebrate and wish him well. Earle sells his cow, Blossom, to Roger Deering for $75 and gives his mother the money. Ma assures Earle that God will bring him back safely. Ma knits an afghan blanket for Earle using her favorite colors from the aurora borealis in the Norwegian sky. The family tries to keep a check on their emotions, but they are all proud of Earle.

June 4. 1944—Allied forces enter Rome.

June 5, 1944—Earle reports for duty.

Dad signs up for added hours at the South Portland Shipyard, anxious to end the war sooner.

June 6, 1944—Allied forces invade Normandy in northern France. Germany begins to retreat.

Earle takes the train from Portland to South Station, Boston, then on to Parris Island, South Carolina, for basic training. Sgt. Patch is the drill instructor. He is from Waterville, Maine, and asks if any of the recruits are from Maine. Earle and four others raise their hands. Sgt. Patch makes them all squad leaders. Patch then asks how many of them grew up on farms; several more raise their hands, so he makes all of them team leaders. Patch says he has no use for any of the city boys because they don't know how to shoot or work long hours.

The Marine recruits begin their training with many long marches in the woods using a map and compass and learning hand-to-hand combat with a bayonet. They practice shooting on a firing range. Earle qualifies for twelve weapons, one of which is a rifle. During training, recruits have to shoot a flag on a pole as quickly as they can, then proceed to the next flag, doing the same thing. It definitely reminds Earle of killing partridge and woodcock back home.

Earle believes he is in good shape when the serial number on his rifle begins with his lucky number 22. He carries that same M1 rifle, serial number 2246495, from training at Parris Island to Camp Lajeune, North Carolina, to Camp Pendleton, California, and later to Maui, where he joins his unit in the Fleet Marine Force, 4th Marine Division, 3rd Battalion, 25th Marines.

Earle Norris Ahlquist in his Marine Corps uniform, 1944.

After six weeks of training, Earle takes a train across country to Camp Pendleton, where he undergoes more training to prepare for war in the Pacific. He is assigned to the 25th Marine Regiment, 4th Division, 3rd Battalion, Company B. Earle is a squad leader. Boarding a Liberty Ship the young Marines head to the South Pacific.

June, 1944—Flonnie turns 20 and can legally join the service. Her parents give their approval.

July 10, 1944—Karine accompanies Flonnie to Boston by train, where they locate the recruitment office. Flonnie signs up for the Women Accepted for Volunteer Emergency Services (WAVES) of the Navy. Rudolph and Marjorie Ahlquist celebrate their 21st anniversary on this date.

Florence L. Ahlquist in her WAVE uniform, 1944.

July 19 1944—Marines invade Guam in the Marianas.

July 24, 1944—Marines invade Tinian in the Marianna Islands. Tinian becomes the storage depot for American bombs. Earle is part of special group selected to protect the storage area. Peter Rogers, son of George Rogers (of Rogers' Bakery) is a key man in protecting the storage area. Earle becomes close to fellow Marine Hainey Wilson of Florence, South Carolina. They dream of going to Alaska when the war ends. Earle is assigned to work closely with Lt. Archibald "Joe" Chambers of West Virginia. Lt. Chambers has watched Earle closely and decides he needs him close by if combat gets intense.

August 24, 1944—Flonnie reports for boot camp at Hunter College, 68th Street and Lexington, Bronx, New York for six weeks.

October 6, 1944—Flonnie returns home for one week before reporting for further training. When she gets there, she is greeted by younger sister Paulie dressed in a uniform that matches the one worn by her big sister. Mama has sewn a miniature matching uniform for nine-year-old Paulie, much to Paulie's delight and Flonnie's surprise.

October 13, 1944—Flonnie reports for special training at Fairchild Aeronautical Company in New York City, staying at Hunter College. After six months of training learning how to repair cameras, she becomes a Specialist, 2nd Class, V-10. She finishes first in her class at the Aerial Camera Repair School and as a result can choose the base (in the United States) where she will serve. She chooses Corpus Christi, Texas. The armed forces has begun to map pictures from the air, and Flonnie becomes part of the early team to work on these specialized cameras.

Late summer through fall, 1944—The 25th Marine Regiment takes control of several Japanese occupied islands: Eniwetok in the Marshall Islands and Saipan and Tinian, two of the Marianna Islands. All contain important air bases vital to breaking Japanese control of the South Pacific. Earle continues arduous training on

Paulie and Flonnie in matching uniforms, 1944.

Maui. Major General Clifton Cates is the division commander. He places great emphasis on competitive sports; all are strongly encouraged to participate. Earle tries boxing, but decides he isn't suited to the sport, though he does well at it. Instead he joins the football team. Although he has never played the sport before, he soon realizes he is a natural left-footed kicker. The coach, a lieutenant colonial who formerly coached at Boston University, leads an incredible team. They are undefeated; only one team manages to score points against them. They rack up a total of 164 points to 6 for their opponents. Hawaii's *Island Breeze* newspaper describes the team as, "one of the greatest football teams we have ever seen at the professional, collegiate or service levels." They are the South Pacific champions, and the team's players are offered scholarships after the war.

Earle enjoys playing on the team, but, as he later discovers, the most important asset from that time is his friendship with the team doctor, a Coast Guard lieutenant colonel who thought highly of Earle.

Earle Ahlquist in Hawaii, Christmas, 1944.

CHAPTER 35
Maui

The interlude at Hawaii gave the Marines a break before they hit the other islands in the South Pacific. During that time Major General Clifton Cates kept them all busy with highly competitive sports activities, football in particular.

Earle found that he thoroughly enjoyed the sport. It felt good to receive the accolades he won for his football acumen—there was no doubt about that.

Soon after arriving in Maui, Earle was promoted to corporal. He decided to go out that night and celebrate with friends Haney Wilson and Sam Cooper. They walked by one of the bars in town and saw a sign on the front: "Only Navy personnel allowed, no Marines."

Earle, Haney, and Sam had already consumed a few beers. They looked at each other. They looked at the sign and simultaneously decided they had to rectify the situation and educate the sailors inside the bar.

The three Marines walked in, took down the sign, then systematically cleaned out the place of nine sailors. One of them took over duties at the bar.

They stayed there all night and missed formation the next morning.

When they got back to base, the officers brought Earle to the colonel and read off the charges.

The colonel looked at Earle and said, "Ahlquist, I see you recently made corporal."

"Yes, Sir," Earle responded.

"Well, I see you haven't sewed the rank on your shirt yet," the colonel said.

"No, Sir," said Earle.

"Well," the colonel said, "I'm going to save you the trouble."

Earle didn't really care. He'd had fun the night before, and he figured where they were going rank wasn't going to matter much.

CHAPTER 36
WAVES: Women Serve, Too

The creation of the WAVES, the women's branch of the United States Naval Reserve during World War II, stirred controversy but left a legacy of accomplishment. It was established by an act of Congress on July 21, 1942, in large measure through the efforts of Dr. Margaret Chung, a noted physician; First Lady Eleanor Roosevelt; and members of the Navy's Women's Advisory Council. The act of Congress authorized the Navy to accept women into the naval reserve as commissioned officers and at the enlisted level, effective for the duration of the war plus six months. The aim was to assign women to shore duties, thereby releasing men in those positions for active sea duty.

Officer candidates had to be between 20 and 49 years old with a college degree, or two years of college and two years of equivalent professional experience. Enlisted WAVES had to be age 20 to 35, with a high school or business diploma or equivalent work experience.

WAVES recruitment posters hung by the South Portland Shipyard gates were readily visible to employees and those walking nearby. Recruitment calls were featured on the radio and news reels at local theaters. The idea that women could enlist to free up more men to serve in combat —and end the fighting—began to gain traction in a public weary of the war. Once families felt assured their daughters would be treated respectfully and would be doing important work, they became less resistant to letting them serve. Even so, many still held onto the notion that women's place was at home, not serving in the military.

Wanting to do her part, Flonnie decided to enlist. She reported to boot camp on August 24, 1944. The Ahlquist family held their own varying views on the subject. Dad and Mama stood behind Flonnie's desire to serve, however. They were confident of her ability to make solid, moral choices in her selection of friends and activities. They knew her skills were needed to aid the armed forces, a fact she had demonstrated at the shipyard; and they fervently prayed the initiative to enlist women would shorten the war. When others expressed opposition to the idea of women in the military, they stood firm in their faith in the Lord and their daughter, and Ma and Pa stood with them. Soon cousin Frances also joined the WAVES; cousin Althea would follow in their footsteps, serving during the Korean Conflict.

Hunter College in New York City became boot camp for Flonnie. Except for arms training, many aspects of the WAVES training resembled that experienced at the men's boot camp. Strict regulations were set in place concerning dress, conduct, and physical health. Flonnie's pageboy hairstyle was cut to shoulder length, and she was instructed to keep it up off her shoulders, away from her face, and in an attractive yet modest style. Each recruit was given two sets of uniforms with appropriate shoes, hats, gloves, purses, and coats—one set for winter, one for summer. The sharply dressed WAVES were expected to conduct themselves in a respectful manner.

The day began with reveille at 5:30 A.M., breakfast at 6:30, and classes and drill for four hours before lunch. Afternoon classes and drills lasted for another four hours. The recruits had an hour of free time before dinner and two hours of study or instruction before lights out at 10 P.M. After captain's inspection on Saturday mornings, the women had free time until taps. Sundays began with reveille at 7 A.M. with breakfast at 7:30, then church services and free time until 7:30 P.M., when study hours began. They learned discipline and pride in their ability to help in the war effort as they marched in formation and sang the song of the WAVES, written by Betty St. Clair and Elizabeth Ender to harmonize with the Navy's anthem, "Anchors Aweigh."

After testing, the WAVES were divided into special areas of training. Many of the women became clerks, cooks, medical aides, and members of the nursing corps. A few became mechanics. Flonnie joined a select few who underwent specialized training in aerial camera repair. The military had just begun to use aerial cameras. As with most new technology, the

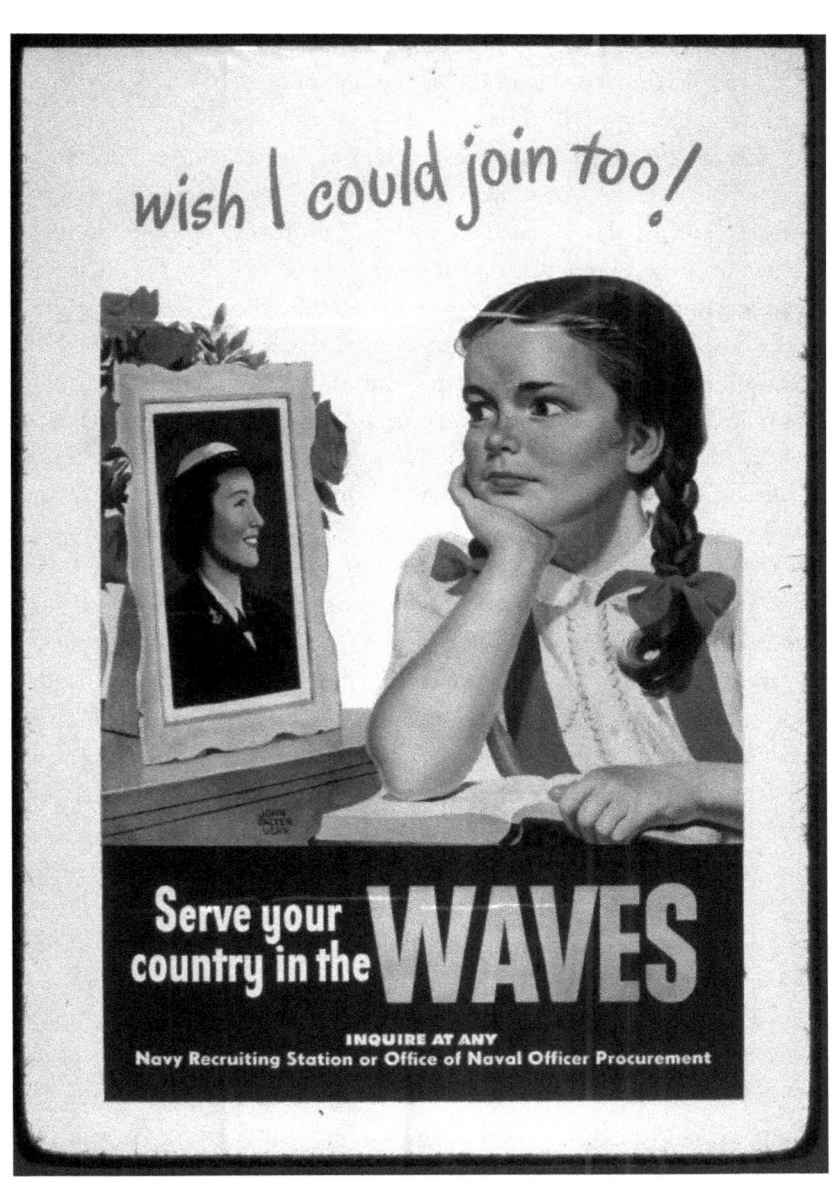

Waves recruiting poster during World War II.

cameras often broke down and required specialized repairs—sometimes by trial and error—to keep them in working order. They were very heavy and cumbersome, yet intricate.

Flonnie proved to be unusually adept at meeting the technical challenges the new cameras presented. After completing boot camp at Hunter College, she was assigned to six months of intense training at Fairchild Aeronautical School on 10th Avenue in New York City. She lived at Hunter College and commuted to the school, where both men and women received instruction in camera repair. Fairchild, a pioneer in aerial photography, made the firm's knowledge and training available to the military for aerial surveillance during World War II. As early as 1935 the federal government had contracted with Fairchild to procure aerial images of the United States. Dad and Mama had given their permission to allow Fairchild to take aerial pictures of their farm and land.

Flonnie's skill in reading patterns for knitted and crocheted wear, which in turn developed into an ability to translate blueprints into ships, laid the perfect groundwork for dealing with the intricately built, yet cumbersome cameras. Coming from a farm family that often had to innovate, she proved to be a capable and quick learner. She graduated at the top of her class, which earned her the privilege of choosing where she would serve in the United States. She chose the Naval Air Base of Corpus Christi, Texas, located on the Gulf of Mexico. Established only four years previously, the base trained pilots and needed camera repair technicians.

Taking a train across country, Flonnie arrived at the base in late spring 1945 and began to settle in. She was the only woman on a team of 39 men who dealt with the cameras. She wrote home to Mama and Dad that it was like having 39 brothers instead of just three. Unlike having seniority at home as the eldest sibling, she had to earn her place among the other repair technicians---which she accomplished with skill and clear capability. They soon respected her work and no-nonsense style. Her commanding officer and co-workers were impressed with her innovation and skill as she used alternative materials, like baling wire, to perform tricky repairs and create broken parts. With the lack of replacement parts, innovation became a necessity, and Flonnie became highly valued

142

for her creative solutions to problems. She often visited local junk yards to scrounge for parts that could be adapted to fix broken cameras. Those years of reworking parts on the farm proved valuable lessons.

Letters back and forth from Scarborough to Corpus Christi were frequent. Mama had seen a new book at the library for 100 recipes for chicken. She wrote Flonnie that she was confident her daughter could author a book about 100 ways to use chicken wire.

The men on the team all came to look upon Flonnie as their sister, friend, co-worker and sometimes model as they tried out their cameras. They also became her guardians, insisting on screening every sailor who tried to date her.

One particular sailor, Gerald Link, was able to pass muster with the tight-knit team of co-workers. Jerry, originally from Patterson, New Jersey, was eight years older than Florence. He had already served for several years in the Seabees and had been stationed in Trinidad, where the Seabees built Army and Naval bases. Trinidad, a British island off the coast of Venezuela, reported sightings in 1941 of German U-boats intent on disrupting shipping in the Caribbean. Under an agreement with Great Britain, the United States sent the Seabees to the island to build observatory stations, air bases, and barracks for the American troops who were charged with protecting the strategic area.

When Jerry's enlistment was up in the Seabees, he chose to re-enlist in the Navy and became a ship's cook. He knew the way to soften resistance from Flonnie's "brothers" was to come bearing gifts of food, which was exactly what he did. Jerry met Flonnie through her best friend in the WAVES, Lorraine Henderson, who was a clerk on the base. She introduced Jerry to Flonnie, and with very careful planning, Jerry made sure he brought plenty of snacks to keep her co-workers occupied and happy so he could date this tall, blue-eyed blonde who had definitely caught his attention.

Jerry successfully pursued Flonnie, and they were married June 16, 1946, at the chapel at Corpus Christie, Texas. Flonnie completed her work with the WAVES and was honorably discharged on February 12, 1947. She had attained the rank of Specialist, 2nd Class V-10. She had served two and one-half years. Women serving in the military were not

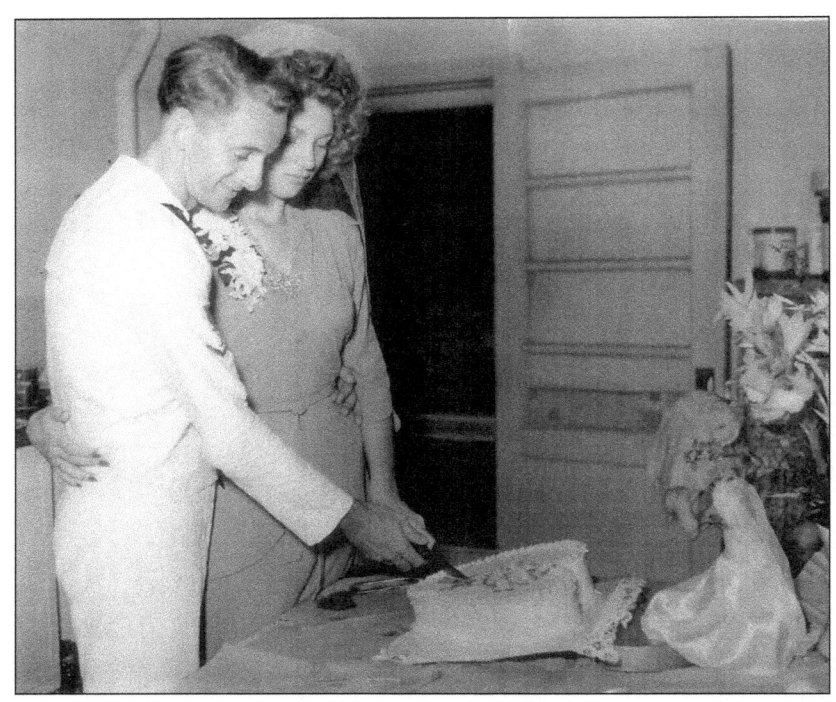

Gerald Link and Florence Ahlquist Link at their wedding in 1946.

supposed to be married, but the war had officially ended on September 2, 1945, and she had served well. After Jerry served the remaining few months to complete his military assignment, Flonnie would be free to return home to Maine.

CHAPTER 37
Stars Guide the Way

On February 17, 1945, Earle's transport ship silently anchored offshore Iwo Jima. It was the dead of night. The Marines onboard knew they were about to launch an important offensive. Their transport ship was one of many, all starting to surround the island. They had been clearing the islands all along the South Pacific to isolate the Japanese and cripple their air bases. Iwo Jima held three important air bases and was within striking distance of Japan. The island had been repeatedly hit with air offensives for months but remained active. The Marines held tight and considered how to approach things. Iwo Jima was a volcanic island with beaches composed of hard gray ash. Major General Clifton Cates and his staff decided they needed a scouting party to survey the island at night. Five Marines were selected for this task; Earle was among the five.

The mission was clear: proceed in complete silence, gather whatever information they could, concentrating on beaches 1 and 2, and return well before dawn. With no weapons except knives, they proceeded to the island. The five Marines understood the mission, but two of them expressed their misgivings simultaneously: "We can do the mission, but finding our way back is the real problem." Earle looked up at the stars, imbued with a strong sense that Pa was right there with him, and said confidently, "I can find our way back." Surprised but trusting Earle's abilities, the others said, "Okay, we'll follow you."

Earle remembered the many evenings he had spent with his grandfather as the older man instructed him in celestial navigation. He looked up again and memorized the location of key stars as the scouting party slipped onto a flat wooden raft and wordlessly paddled to within 500 feet of the coast of Iwo Jima, silently moving through sharks and alli-

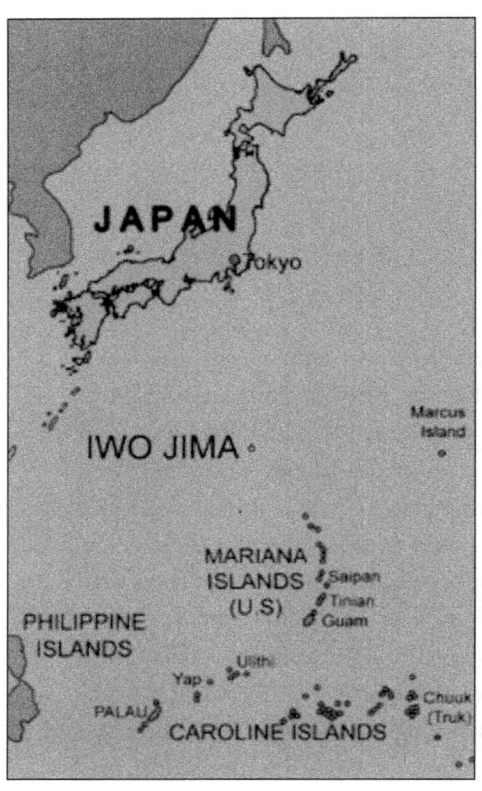

Map of Iwo Jima.

gators as they went. Two Marines remained with the raft as three men quietly slipped into the water and swam to the island to gather the required information.

One of the first things Earle discovered was a piece of smashed equipment abandoned on the beach. The equipment was designed to remove salt from ocean water to provide water for drinking. From this, he deduced that the Japanese were likely short of drinking water. Other parts of the shoreline were littered with military debris damaged from the U.S. air raids. After gathering information about the location of bunkers and holdings and watching the sky, the team headed back to the ship. As silently as they had come, the Marines navigated through the dangerous waters to join their comrades. Earle's ability to travel by celestial navigation proved invaluable. Through it all, Earle had the clear sensation that Pa stood beside him—it was as if his grandfather had prepared him for this very moment. Earle was humbled when he remembered what an impatient student he had been. He recalled Ma's words when she reassured him that God would be with him: "When you pass through the waters I will be with you; and through the rivers, they shall not overwhelm you; when you walk through the fire you shall not be burned." The verse came from Isaiah in the Bible, but Earle didn't know that at the time. All he knew was that the words proved literally true that night.

Two days later the U.S. Marines invaded Iwo Jima.

CHAPTER 38
Iwo Jima and Near Death

In early 1945, Earle's unit, the 25th Marines, along with thousands of other Marines boarded ships and left Maui to join the fight against the Japanese in the Pacific. They took zigzag routes so as not to alert the enemy where they were going. The Marines themselves didn't know their destination until a few days before they arrived.

Their mission was to take control of the island of Iwo Jima, which measured two miles wide and four miles long. The 3rd, 4th, and 5th Marine Divisions would land on the island—in all, more than 60,000 men. Earle would be among the first wave of Marines to land. His unit, the 25th Marines, 3rd Battalion would have the most difficult mission, landing on what the Marines called "Blue Beach."

The date for the invasion was set for Monday, February 19. The Marines were told it would be a "cakewalk"—72 hours at the most. Based on the enemy's past performance, military strategists expected that the Marines' frontal assault would be met in kind. The Japanese had no coastline defenses in place, leading the Americans to believe there were far fewer Japanese troops than there were. What Allied troops discovered later was the deep network of tunnels the Japanese had constructed to protect their troops and defend the island. The tunnels and natural caves hid about 21,000 enemy soldiers.

While preparing to board the amphibious landing craft, Earle was struck with the impressive number of American ships surrounding him contrasted with the utter quiet of the beach. No birds flew overhead. The stillness, however, was short-lived.

Earle's vessel sailed for shore, among the first wave heading to Blue Beach Two. Before the boat could land, an explosion of bullets from

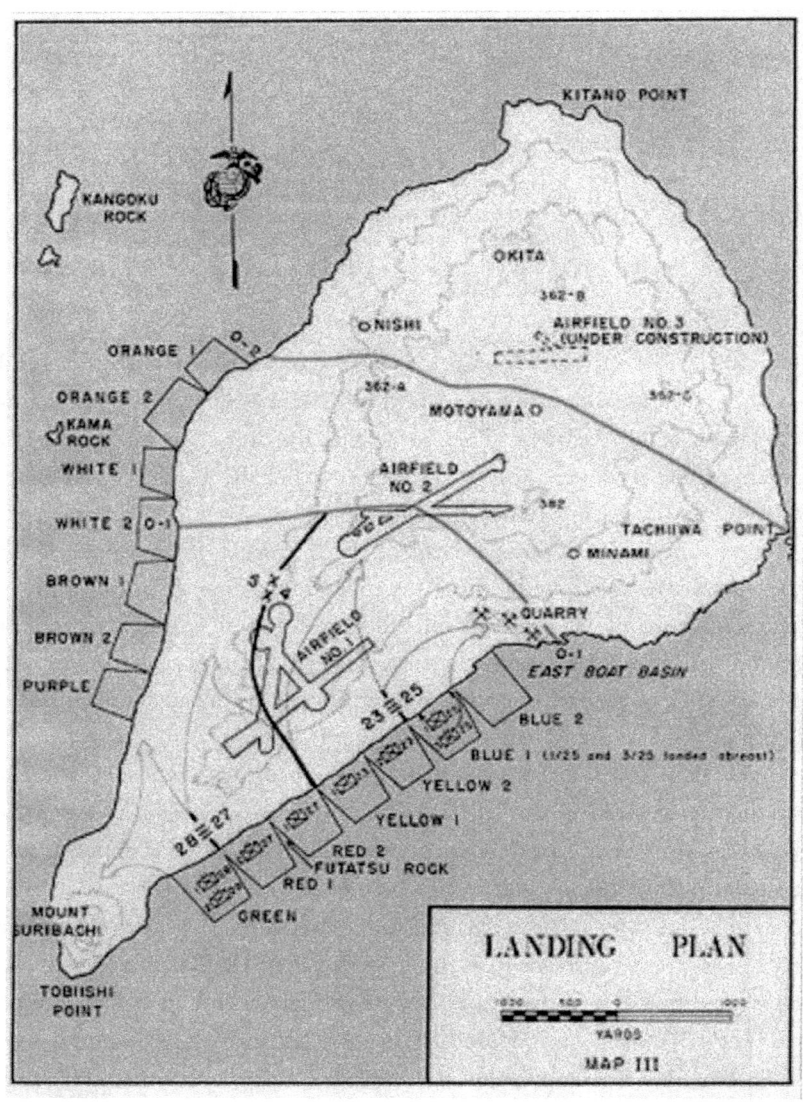

Iwo Jima landing plan

148

the island hammered Earle's craft, and it started to sink. His squad was quickly shifted to a passing craft that had just deposited troops. It turned to land the 4th Division, only to be hit too. As the craft began to sink, Earle went into action. He and his fellow Marines swam ashore carrying their 100-pound packs. Earle shrugged off his load of arms, swam back to help others, and began pulling fellow Marines sinking under their loads. He flung about twelve of them to safety before he scrambled back to seek cover from another barrage of bullets. His good friend Sam Cooper suddenly stood up and faced the enemy, yelling, "Come and get me!" Earle immediately turned and knocked Sam down. Huddling together, they began firing at the enemy.

On February 19, 1945, the combatants endured some of the fiercest and bloodiest fighting of the war in the Pacific. The battle would continue almost nonstop for five weeks until March 29. Fighting continued day and night as the Marines penetrated the Japanese strongholds. They soon realized that the Japanese had built eleven miles of intricate tunnels and camouflaged artillery positions. Easing himself into a small foxhole for protection, Earle distinctly heard Japanese voices beneath him. He quickly moved.

Finally American tanks came ashore to provide cover, and the troops were able to move inland. One Marine observed, "At great cost, you'd take a hill to find then the same enemy suddenly on your flank or rear. The Japanese were not on Iwo Jima. They were in it!"

The Japanese seemed to anticipate where Americans would strike next. Each foray up the hills was met with a barrage of enemy fire. The Marines soon dubbed the area, halfway up the island and surrounded by the enemy's tunnels, "the meatgrinder," and limited their attacks to nighttime when darkness provided cover.

Earle's battalion landed approximately 900 men on the morning of February 19 and immediately ran into what Marine General Clifton Cates later called a "buzz saw of automatic gunfire from the Japanese." By nightfall, only 150 Marines remained in fighting condition, an almost incredible 83.3% casualty rate. An additional 30,000 Marines landed that night, followed by 40,000 more men.

On Friday, February 23, the Marines took Mount Suribachi and mounted a flag there to show American ships at sea that U.S. troops had control of a strategic location. Ship's horns sounded celebratory blasts as flares went up. Later a larger flag was flown in the same location, replacing the smaller flag planted at the site. Earle saw both events and though fighting remained intense, he and his fellow Marines took heart. Earle was one of a handful left from the original landing force who remained when they overtook the airstrip on Iwo Jima. They knew the battle was far

U.S. flag over Mount Suribachi

from over, but their resolve was firm: they would complete their mission, and they would stay alive.

There seemed to be no let-up in the fighting. The men could take only short cat naps when a fellow Marine could cover for them. Looking up, a startled Earle saw a Japanese soldier with a bayonet charging toward him. The bayonet lodged in his left hand as he tried to fend it off. The eyes of the enemy were chilling as Earle quickly pulled his gun and fired, killing the soldier.

Haney and Sam looked at Earle and said, "You need a medic."

Earle shook his head. Tearing off part of his shirt, he wrapped his left hand tightly to stop the bleeding. He wasn't going to leave his crew.

The men constantly sprinted through a barrage of fire. On February 28 Earle was on his way to a supply depot to refill his ammunition when he was hit by a rocket. Shrapnel lodged in his shoulder, and the bone in his left leg shattered. Seven nearby Marines were killed. Medics were under fire as they tried to evacuate him. He rolled into the woods for cover before the medics were able to get him safely to a hospital ship in the harbor. Earle had eleven wounds in all, most of which were in his left leg and right shoulder. He was evacuated to a Coast Guard ship offshore, where medics told him his left leg would have to be amputated. Relief swept over Earle when he saw that the surgeon in charge was his former football team doctor, who recognized Earle and promised to try to save his leg.

Earle's left foot had been shot off and several bones shattered. Earle lay back and tried to rest, realizing he had almost died, but relieved he had a friend in this doctor. He believed Ma's promise that God would take care of him and bring him home.

From the Coast Guard ship, Earle went to a field hospital in Guam, where his shoulder was well bandaged and splints applied to his leg. The doctor had managed to reattach his foot. From Guam he was transported to the hospital at Pearl Harbor, Hawaii. Doctors there put him in a cast from the hip to the ball of his foot to totally immobilize the leg.

While at the Pearl Harbor hospital, Earle had a surprise visitor. Margaret Chase Smith, Congresswoman from Maine, came to his bedside. She was visiting with all the soldiers from Maine. She kindly asked him what she could do for him. Amazed and touched, Earle told her that he wished she could contact his folks in Scarborough, Maine, and let them know he had been hurt, but that he was okay. He would get well.

Representative Smith (later to serve as a U.S. Senator) promptly did just that, phoning them as soon as she was able. This was the first news Dad and Mama had of what had happened. Public reports had been severely limited, and personal letters were edited so as not to endanger the troops if they were intercepted. From the newsreels at the theaters and broadcasts over the radio, Dad and Mama suspected that Earle was part of the fighting in the Pacific, but they did not know details. Flonnie, from her military position in Texas, was able to gain some insight, but even that was limited. Margaret Chase Smith's reassuring report from Earle greatly relieved the family. Thereafter, they would receive regular reports as Earle was transferred from one military hospital to another.

On March 26, 1945, the Allies, led by the U.S. Marines, captured Iwo Jima. The battle claimed 6,821 American soldiers and wounded 19,217. Japan lost 18, 375 soldiers; 216 were taken prisoner.

Later, Marine correspondent S/Sgt David Dempsey reported,

"Something that has been forgotten: there are places where there is no use sending bombs and shells to do a job. Instead you must send men, alone and willing to die...."

"Among the Americans who served on Iwo Island, uncommon valor was a common virtue," Admiral Chester Nimitz noted in his final communique, which appeared in *Life* magazine's April 9, 1945, issue.

On April 12, 1945, President Franklin Delano Roosevelt died, and Harry S. Truman became President of the United States of America.

Resting in his Pearl Harbor hospital room, Earle heard the news. Shortly afterward, he (along with many other wounded Marines) boarded a ship to San Francisco. From there, they would travel to a variety of stateside hospitals. Earle, not one to stay still, had become accustomed to the full-length cast on his left leg. Nurses aboard the transport ship kept chiding him for wandering about the ship and not staying in his bunk. But he was agitated and anxious not only about those he had left behind but about his future as well. Suddenly he heard a familiar voice call out his name. He followed the call, and pulling back a curtain he spotted his good friend Sam Cooper. Looking down at the cot, he saw that Sam had lost both legs and an arm. Earle said, "Looks like you've been hit pretty hard, Sam."

"It's nothing, Earle," replied Sam. "I am alive! And I've got a lot of living yet to do. I will just do it differently now."

Immediately, Earle no longer felt sorry for himself or anxious about how he would face tomorrow.

On May 8, 1945, Europe celebrated Victory Day, but fighting continued in the Pacific.

From San Francisco, Earle traveled to a Norfolk, Virginia, hospital for a lengthy rehabilitation. By then an expert at manipulating his leg cast, Earle explored his surroundings. The nurses had a hard time keeping up with him. Grateful to be alive, Earle kept himself busy doing jobs for others. Pa had always said, "If you can't be ornamental, you better become useful." One day, while Earle was repairing windows at a cottage several nurses had rented, a messenger hailed him and told him to get back to the hospital for something important.

He walked in, swinging his encased left leg, to be greeted by Mama,

Aunt Harriette, and Ma. They had taken a train from Maine to see him and confer with the doctors. Earle, thrilled by the visit, was thankful that he was up and about when they arrived. Ma and Mama, surprised by Earle's agility and greatly relieved, chuckled at this enterprising boy of theirs. After visiting with Earle and bringing him tins of homemade cookies, they made an appointment with the doctors to hear what he was facing.

Doctors changed the cast every month, and each part of the leg was evaluated. The bones had been badly broken, the ankle was severely damaged, and the left foot had been reattached—each part healed at its own pace. The cast ensured that the joints were totally immobilized to promote healing. Fortunately, Earle's hobbling about had not compromised that and did wonders for his outlook. They all understood that this would be a lengthy process and if infection set in any time along the path to recovery, he was in danger of losing his leg.

During their interview with the doctors, the women emphasized the importance of saving Earle's leg. After a few days, they headed back home, much relieved to have seen Earle and with a much brighter outlook. Earle continued to improve, aware of his mother's and grandmother's warnings not to endanger the leg further, but recognizing his own need for heathy activity.

On August 6, 1945, the United States dropped an atomic bomb on Hiroshima, Japan. Three days later, a second atomic bomb was dropped on Nagasaki, Japan. After having fought the Japanese at Iwo Jima, the recovering Marines at the Norfolk hospital absolutely believed that this maneuver shortened the war and ultimately saved lives, though they all agreed it was an awesome, even awful, move.

On August 14, 1945 (U.S. time), Japan surrendered, and on September 2, 1945, Japan signed the formal document officially ending World War II.

At the end of September, Earle traveled to Philadelphia for an evaluation by doctors at the VA facility there before getting final clearance to go home. On October 5, he received his discharge from the U.S. Marine Corps and a train ticket home to Portland Maine.

The following day, a Saturday, Earle shook himself awake as the train pulled in to Union Station in Portland. He disembarked, walking with a cane and carrying his small duffle bag. At the bus station, the driver, Jack Straw, Earle's former 4-H coach, greeted him.

Earle said, "I don't have any money."

"No matter," Mr. Straw responded. "Climb aboard, Earle. This one's on me."

At Earle's request, the bus dropped him off at the Star Theater in Westbrook, where Earle knew family members would be watching the latest news reels and a feature film. He walked into the darkened theater, as yet unnoticed by the other movie patrons. As he came down the aisle, he spotted cousin Donna and his little sister, Paulie, sitting with Ma and Pa. Uncle Dick had brought them. The Tarzan movie was soon forgotten, eclipsed by the overwhelming joy of having their Earle back home after many long months of worry and waiting. Tears glistened Ma and Pa's eyes. Riding back to the farm, Paulie snuggled next to her brother and a relieved quiet settled on them all.

After giving a warm hug to Mama, Earle headed to the barn to see Dad, who was finishing up with the cows. As Dad turned and saw his son standing there, Earle was struck at how much his father had aged in the eighteen months of his absence. He looked 10 years older than when Earle had seen him last.

Father and son hugged and wept together. "I always knew you'd come home," Dad said.

Then Chub bounded in. The circle was complete.

The following Monday, Earle returned to Scarborough High School. With his cane for support, he walked into Principal Bessey's office to sign up for classes. He had a year and a half to complete for his graduation, then on to college.

Elwood Bessey was relieved to see his student/athlete walk into his office. They agreed Earle could double up on some classes in order to complete his requirements in time for graduation in June. Though Earle could no longer run track and field, he did join the rifle club and was sometimes called upon to substitute for the math teacher.

As he emerged from Principal Bessey's office, he was greeted in the hallway by longtime friend Winonah Bowley, who quickly planted a kiss on his cheek as she hugged him and welcomed him home.

Earle and Winonah, 1946

Surprised, he looked down at her and smiled. My goodness, she had grown up, he thought.

They were married the following November.

Appendix: Christmas Poems and Recipes

Annie's and Willie's Prayer
written by Sophia P. Snow

Twas the eve before Christmas. Good night had been said
And Annie and Willie had crept into bed.
There were tears on their pillows and tears in their eyes
And each little bosom was heaving with sighs.
For tonight their stern father's command had been given
That they should retire precisely at seven,
Instead of at eight, for they troubled him more
With questions unheard of than ever before.
He told them he thought this delusion a sin,
No such person as Santa Claus ever had been
And he hoped after this he would never more hear
How he scrambled down chimneys with presents each year.
And this was the reason that two little heads
So restlessly tossed on their soft downy beds.

Eight, nine and the clock had struck ten
Not a word had been spoken by either 'til then
When Willie's sad face from the blanket did peep
And whispered, "Dear Annie, is you fast asleep?"
"Why, no, brother Willie," a sweet voice replied.
"I've long tried in vain, but I can't shut my eyes.
For somewhere it makes me so sorry because,
Dear Papa has said there is no Santa Claus.
Now we know that there is. It can't be denied,

He came every year before Mama died.
But then I have been thinking that she used to pray
And God would hear everything Mama would say
 And perhaps she asked him to send Santa Claus here
With a sack full of presents he brought every year.

Well, why can't we pray, just as Mama did then
And ask him to send him with presents again?"
"I've been thinking so too." And without a word more
Four little bare feet bounded out on the floor
Four little knees the soft carpet pressed
And two tiny hands were close to each breast.
"Now Willie, you know we must firmly believe
That the presents we ask for we will surely receive.
You must wait just as still, 'til I say the Amen.
By that you will know your turn has come then."

"Dear Jesus, look down on my brother and me
And grant us the favor we are asking of thee.
I want a wax dolly, a tea set and ring
An ebony workbox that shuts with a spring.
Bless Papa, Dear Jesus, and cause him to see
That Santa Claus loves us as much as does he.
Don't let him get fretful and angry again
At dear brother Willie and Annie again. Amen."
"Please Deasus, let Santa Taus tum down tonight
And bring us some presents before it is light.
I want he should give me a nice little sled
With bite shiny runners and all painted red,
A box full of tandy, a book and a toy.
Amen, and then Deasus, I'll be a dood boy.

Their prayers being ended, they raised up their heads
And with hearts light and cheerful again sought their bed.
They were soon lost in slumber both peaceful and deep

And with faeries in dreamland were roaming in sleep.
Eight,nine and the little French clock had struck ten
'Ere the father had thought of the children again.
He seemed to hear Annie's half suppressed sighs
And to see the big tears stand in Willie's blue eyes
I was harsh with my darlings he mentally said
And should not have sent them so early to bed.
But then was trouble my feelings found vent
For the bank stocks today had gone down ten percent
But they have forgotten their troubles 'ere this
And I had denied the twice asked for kiss
But just to make sure, I'll steal up to their door
For I never spoke harsh to my darlings before.

So saying, he softly ascended the stairs
And arrived at their door to hear both of their prayers.
His Annie's. "Bless Papa" drew forth the big tear
And Willie's grave promise fell sweet on his ear.
Strange, strange, I'd forgotten, said he with a sigh
How I longed as a child to have Christmas draw nigh.
I'll atone for my harshness, he inwardly said
By answering their prayer ere I sleep in my bed.
Then he turned to the stairs and softly went down
Threw off velvet slippers and silk dressing gown
Donned hat, coat and boots and was out on the street
A millionaire facing the cold, driving sleet

Nor stopped he until he had bought every thing
From a box full of candy to a tiny gold ring
Indeed he kept adding so much to his store
That the various presents outnumbered a score.
Then homeward he turned with his holiday load
And with Aunt Mary's help in the nursery was stowed.
Miss dolly was seated beneath a pine tree,
By the side of a table spread out for her tea.

A workbox well filled in the center was laid,
And on it the ring for which Annie had prayed
A soldier in uniform stood by the sled
With bright shining runners, and all painted red.
There were balls, dogs and horses, books pleasing to see,
And birds of all colors were perched in the tree
While Santa Claus , laughing, stood up in the top
As if, getting ready more presents to drop.

And as the picture the fond father surveyed,
He thought for his trouble, he had amply been paid.
And he said to himself as he brushed off a tear,
I'm happier tonight then I've been for a year.
What care I if bank stocks fell ten percent more;
Hereafter, I'll make it a rule I believe,
To have Santa Claus visit us each Christmas eve.
So saying, he gently extinguished the light,
Then tripping down stairs to retire for the night.
As soon as the beams of the bright morning sun
Put the darkness to flight, and the stars one by one
Four little blue eyes out of sleep opened wide,
And at the same moment the presents they spied.
Then out of their beds they sprang with a bound
And all the gifts prayed for were all of them found.
They laughed and they cried in their innocent glee
And shouted for Papa to come quick and see.
What presents of Santa brought in the night,
Just the things that they wanted and left before light;
And now added Annie in a voice soft and low,
"You'll believe there's a Santa Claus, Papa, I know."
While dear little Willie climbed up on his knee,
Determined no secret between them there would be
And told in soft whispers how Annie had said
That their dear blessed Mama, so long ago dead,
Used to kneel down by the side of her chair

And Dod up in heaven had answered her prayer.
Then we got up and prayed, just as well as we could.
And Dod answered our prayer, now wasn't he dood?"
"I should say that He was if he brought you all these,
And know just what presents my children would please."
Well, well let him think so, the dear little elf
'Twould be cruel to tell him I did it myself.
Blind father, who caused your proud heart to relent,
And the hasty spoken so soon to repent?
'Twas the Being who bade you steal softly upstairs
And made you His agent to answer their prayer.

This was recited by Earle at the Christmas pageant of the Beech Ridge Community School for the Christmas Pageant.

Santa's Cake

I saved my cake for Santy
One Christmas Eve at tea,
For if riding makes one hungry
How hungry he must be!
I put it on the chimney shelf
Where he'd be sure to go.
It does a person good
To be remembered so.
When everyone was fast asleep,
Every one but me.
I tip-toed into Mama's room
Just as still as I could be,
Oh dear, it made my feelings ache,
There sat a miserable little mouse
Eating Santa's cake!

Uncle Nathan Shaw
a poem from Mama's childhood by ??

Now well. Oh woe, Uncle Nathan Shaw,
Funniest old man ever you saw.
At half past four each afternoon.
He'd start a humming an old jig tune.

And take a jug from the pantry shelf,
And trot down cellar to draw himself,
Old cider enough to last through the winter evening.
Two quarts or more as regular as half past four came round.

He'd tackle that cellar door
As he'd done for thirty years or more.
As regular too as he got that jug,
Aunt Shaw would yap, through her cross old mug,
 "Nathan, for goodness sake, take care,
You always slip on that second stair.
Seems as though you'll bust my jug.
Tis the very best there is in town, and you know it too.
It was left me by my great aunt Sue.
For goodness sake, why don't you lug a tin dish down, a-for you break
my jug!"

Always the same for thirty years.
Always the same old twits and jeers.
And still you wonder my friends, at crime,
But Nathan took it slick as a pup,
Always, salesmen, please shut up.
You know what the good folks say
About the preacher went to the old time well.
Rather 'twas that or this time he found,
His stiff old limbs got weak and numb.
Or rather at last his nerves gave in
To Aunt Shaw's ever-lasting whim.

One day he slipped on that second stair,
Whirled around and clutched at the empty air,
And clean to the foot of the stairs—ka-smash!
He bumped the floor with his plump old back.

He scarce struck beneath the final bump,
When old Aunt Shaw she give a jump,
Yelled down the stairs, mad as a bug,
"Now rush my hide, did you bust my jug?"

Not a single word for his poor old bones
Not a word could she hear but his awful groans,
But that blamed old hard-shelled thistle jud,
Wanted to know if her jug was bust.

Old Uncle Nathan lay there flat,
Knocked into the shape of an old cocked hat,
But he got up and brushed off the dirt,
And found after all, he weren't much hurt.

And he saved that jug, his last wild thought had been of that.
He might have caught the cellar shelf, and saved his fall,
But he hung onto that jug through all,

And now, as he loosed his jealous hug,
His wife just screamed, "Did you bust my jug?'
Old Uncle Nathan let out one roar,
Shook his fist at the cellar door,

"Did you bust my jug?" she was screaming still,
"No slam my hide! But I swear I will."
And Ka-flam! You'd thought the house would fall,
When he smashed that jug on the cellar wall.
Like chaff from a threshing floor.

The Village Blacksmith

By Henry Wadsworth Longfellow

Under a spreading chestnut-tree
 The village smithy stands;
The smith, a mighty man is he,
 With large and sinewy hands;
 And the muscles of his brawny arms
 Are strong as iron bands.

His hair is crisp, and black, and long,
 His face is like the tan;
His brow is wet with honest sweat,
 He earns whate'er he can,
And looks the whole world in the face,
 For he owes not any man.

Week in, week out, from morn till night,
 You can hear his bellows blow;
You can hear him swing his heavy sledge,
 With measured beat and slow,
Like a sexton ringing the village bell,
 When the evening sun is low.

And children coming home from school
 Look in at the open door;
They love to see the flaming forge,
 And bear the bellows roar,
And catch the burning sparks that fly
 Like chaff from a threshing-floor.

He goes on Sunday to the church,
 And sits among his boys;
He hears the parson pray and preach,
 He hears his daughter's voice,

Singing in the village choir,
And it makes his heart rejoice.

It sounds to him like her mother's voice,
Singing in Paradise!
He needs must think of her once more,
How in the grave she lies;
And with his hard, rough hand he wipes
A tear out of his eyes.

Toiling,--rejoicing,--sorrowing,
Onward through life he goes;
Each morning sees some task begin,
Each evening sees it close
Something attempted, something done,
Has earned a night's repose.

Thanks, thanks to thee, my worthy friend,
For the lesson thou hast taught!
Thus at the flaming forge of life
Our fortunes must be wrought;
Thus on its sounding anvil shaped
Each burning deed and thought.

CHRISTMAS RECIPES

Jam Thumbprint Cookies

Makes about 3 dozen.

In large bowl sift together 1 ½ cups flour with ¼ teaspoon salt. Set aside. Then in smaller bowl mix 2/3 cup butter and 1/3 cup sugar. Mix until light and fluffy. Then add to this 2 egg yolks and 1 teaspoon vanilla. Beat well. Gradually add this to the dry ingredients and chill about 1 hour. After this, shape the dough into small (about 1 inch) balls. Roll each ball into the 2 egg whites then in ¾ cup finely chopped walnuts. Press a thumbprint into each cookie and put on baking tin.

Bake about 12-15 minutes in moderate oven. Cool on wire rack and fill each thumbprint with cherry, strawberry or raspberry jam. YUMMY. These were favorites of Lee and Paulie.

Sugar Cookies
Makes about 4 dozen

In large bowl cream 1/3 cup butter with 1/3 cup lard until fluffy. Gradually add 1 cup flour, ¾ cup sugar, 1 egg, 1 Tablespoon cream, 1 teaspoon baking powder, 1 teaspoon vanilla and a good dash of salt. Mix well, then add another 1 cup of flour. Divide this dough into two halves and chill a couple hours so that it becomes easy to roll out on a board and cut with cookie cutters. Make sure the board is only lightly floured and roll dough out to about 1/8 inch thick. Cut with a 2 inch cookie cutter and place on ungreased cookie tin. Bake at about 300 degrees for about 7 minutes until set and dry but not brown. Remove onto a wire rack to cool. Then in a smaller bowl mix 1 cup confectioner's sugar with ¼ teaspoon vanilla and a Tablespoon of milk (more if needed—but not much) Then glaze this over the cooled cookies---glaze can be colored or colored sprinkles can be added.

Mama had to make lots of these cookies to keep up with everyone's sweet tooth! Sometimes she would make a double batch of sugar cookies and fill them with jam and press two of them together like little tarts —or cut one a little larger, put a small dab of jam, then press it in half to become a half-round. These need to be baked just a bit longer because they were thicker. The children took turns watching them bake so they would not burn! But it was always yummy!

Julekake
2 cups lukewarm rich milk with 1 yeast cake or 2 packages of dry yeast. Cream together in a big bowl. In separate bowl dissolve 1 cup sugar and 1 cup melted butter. When cooled (so as not to hamper the yeast being active), add to the milk mixture. Slowly add 5 cups of flour with 1 teaspoon cardamom. Mix well. Fold in ½ cup candied currants and ¾ cup raisins. Knead the dough quickly and allow to rest 20 minutes. Be careful to place it in an area with no drafts. Knead again. Shape into

two loaves and allow to rise 30 minutes. Bake in hot oven (375-400 degrees) for 35-40 minutes.

This was traditional Christmas bread; in Norway this was called a Jule Cake. It was fabulous with soft butter.

Buckles

Buckles were a longer process to make. The real name for these cookies was Fattigman, but Mama called them Buckles because that was what they looked like. The dough was made the day before and chilled overnight. The recipe made about 200 cookies, which if not careful could disappear quickly in the household. But because they were a favorite of Dad's Mama always tried to hide a few away in a tin for him to have later. Because it took so many egg yolks, Mama managed to have another recipe available that used the extra egg whites (like and angel food cake or meringue cookies—that always diverted the boys attention, so she could hide some buckles away for Dad!)

Beat 12 egg yolks, 3 egg whites, 1/8 teaspoon salt and 1 1/8 cup sugar together for 30 minutes. Add 1 1/8 cup heavy cream and 1 teaspoon cardamon together. Then add ½ cup melted butter, 1 teaspoon lemon juice and 2 tablespoons brandy. Finally add 7 cups flour that has already been sifted. This dough will be very stiff. Mama often had Flonnie or the boys do some of this stirring. Chill the dough overnight. The next day small amounts of the dough was removed at a time. It was rolled out very thin, almost so you could see the lines on the pastry board. Carefully the dough was cut into diamond shapes with a slit in the center.

Each cookie was quickly fried in hot fat (365 degrees) until lightly brown then quickly removed and put on brown paper to absorb the grease. Sometimes it was rolled in powdered sugar.

Rullepolse

(Ma's meat roll)

Flat meat---about 5 lbs. of venison, beef or pork thinly sliced, about ¼ to 3/8 inch thick

Place meat between layers of waxed paper and pound until very thin.

Mix together in a bowl: 1 tbls. Salt, 1 tbls pepper, 1 tbls ginger

Lay meat flat and evenly spread seasonings over meat—like a dry rub

Grind 1-2 onions in a fine grind and spread over meat.

Roll the meat starting at the short side.

Wrap all in a cheese cloth and tie with twine.

Place all into a large kettle, cover with water, and boil two hours.

Remove from kettle and press between two heavy pans to squeeze out the water. This takes about two hours, sometimes putting weights on the pans helps. Refrigerate. Slice this off to serve at a meal or in sandwiched

Epilogue

A Child's Life 90 Years Ago: Recollections of Florence and Earle *Ahlquist, 1923—1946, Scarborough, Maine,* is as its title suggests, a compilation of remembrances from the first half of the Twentieth Century. The stories take the reader back to a time when the technology we now take for granted completely revolutionized the life of rural Maine farmers.

But these recollections are more than a visit to Norman Rockwell's America. They show how seemingly simple lessons learned on the farm prepared a brother and sister for their parts in events that would change the course of world history. The two siblings witnessed the advent of electricity at the farm, which marked a turning point in the life of its inhabitants. They lived through a Depression, learned how to make do, and earned extra money through their own ingenuity and hard work. And when America called upon its citizens to fight against its enemies, Earle and Florence readily volunteered.

By sharing their memories of these times, they have preserved them for future generations. Incorporated here are the lessons that carried the two through hardships and struggles—ordeals that many of their contemporaries failed to navigate.

What Earle and Florence learned on the farm with their loving, hardworking, close-knit family enabled them to stand proudly shoulder to shoulder with other members of America's Greatest Generation. And they never forgot where they came from.

Florence Ahlquist Link

Jerry and Florence Link settled in Scarborough not far from where Florence grew up and had three daughters, Marjorie, Karen, and Jayne. When Jayne started school, Flonnie went to college to earn a teaching degree.

This was a time when it was rare for married women with a family to be college students. She went on to have a notable career in education and achieved two master's degrees as well. She taught middle school for 25 years, leaving a lasting impact on her students. Aware of the many different ways learning takes place, she introduced Scarborough students to Future Problem Solving, an international academic competition program in which students apply critical thinking and problem-solving skills to hypothetical situations. Her students competed in two national competitions. She and Jerry remained active in First Lutheran Church.

Flonnie continued to "do for others." Her daughters remember falling asleep to the sounds of their mother's sewing machine as it hummed away while she made garments not only for her family but for many others as well. Their home was often the gathering place for the bigger family, whether for casual summertime celebrations or for the family Christmas Eve get-together.

She served as president of the Cumberland County Retired Teachers Association. During summer vacations, she often traveled the world, always urging others to become lifelong learners. Proud of her patriotic heritage, Florence became a member of the local chapter of the Daughters of the American Revolution. She always encouraged good in others and was quick to praise God for all good things that came her way. She met challenges with steady patience.

Growing blindness afflicted Flonnie in her later years, caused by the same malady that had plagued her father and grandfather. She faced it with the same faith they had relied on to get through earlier troubles. She quietly repeated the Twenty-third Psalm and found special meaning in the verse, "Yea, though I walk through the valley of the shadow of death, I will fear no evil: for thou art with me; thy rod and thy staff they comfort me . . . ." She often said that shadows don't kill, they just increase the darkness. But she could deal with the darkness, she said, because "I walk with God."

Mother to three, grandmother to seven, and great-grandmother of eight, Florence was thrilled to have her growing up stories written for family and friends to enjoy. She died in Scarborough on January 16, 2017.

Earle Ahlquist

Earle and Winonah also settled in Scarborough near his childhood home. They had two children, Philip and Earlene. Earle attended Gorham State Teachers College for two years but left to pursue his own business of Ahlquist Builders & Movers Company, where he developed a reputation for tackling challenging jobs. More than once he successfully moved a building across ice during Maine's cold winters. He became one of the primary movers to develop Peary Village in South Portland, Maine.

His passion for hunting and fishing developed into another part-time business as a certified Maine Guide. For thirty-five years he introduced customers to Maine's wilderness with his Allagash River Trips. Baseball hero Ted Williams was among his notable clients.

After retiring from the building moving industry, he continued small construction work. Gaining teacher certification from his many years in business, he taught industrial arts at Biddeford High School.

His response to a neighbor who asked for a loan—part of family lore—reveals his character. Earle told the neighbor, "I won't lend you money, but I will give you the money, because I don't want you avoiding me because you may not be able to pay it back."

After the death of Winonah, Earle married Betty Demmons Haney. They had two children, Oren and Lorraine. Earle is the father of four, grandfather of five, step-grandfather to five, and great-grandfather of fifteen.

A lover of genealogy and family lore, Earle researched and compiled a history of his mother's family, the Paul Chadbourn Family of Waterboro, Maine. He served on the original board of directors for the Chadbourne Family Association and became a charter member of the Maine Nordmenn Lodge for the Sons of Norway. Those interests made him especially gratified to be able to recount his memories of his childhood and young adulthood for family and friends.

Earle died on March 25, 2016.

Notes and Bibliography

This text is based on the author's interviews, interactions, and discussions with Earle Ahlquist and Florence Ahlquist Link over the course of several months in 2016 before their deaths. All recipes and most of the photographs are from the Ahlquist family archives. The poems not otherwise attributed are from memories provided by Earle or Florence. The following attributions are for poems, songs, and illustrations not attained through family records and/or memories.

p. 64, Photograph from the Collections of Haystack Historical Society. Used with permission from the Maine Historical Society.

p. 67, "What God Hath Promised," Flint, Annie Johnson. Text in public domain. Accessed December 31, 2018, https://www.hopepublishing.com/find-hymns-hw/hw4255.aspx#FullDescription

p. 70, "Two Little Boys," Morse, Theodore F, and Edward Madden. *When We Were Two Little Boys*. Howley, Haviland & Dresser, New York, 1903. Notated Music. Accessed December 31, 2018, https://www.loc.gov/item/ihas.100007868/.

p. 72, Photograph from the Collections of Maine Historical Society. Used with permission from the Maine Historical Society.

p. 92, "The Winds of Fate," Ella Wheeler Wilcox. *World Voices*, New York: Hearst's International Library Company, 1916. Text in public domain. Accessed December 31, 2018, http://www.ellawheelerwilcox.org/poems/pwindsof.htm

p. 141, WAVES poster: U.S. National Archives. Accessed Jan. 26, 2019, URL: https://www.flickr.com/photos/usnationalarchives/5532511896.

p. 145-153, "Iwo Jima," Wikipedia. Accessed December 31, 2018, https://en.wikipedia.org/wiki/Iwo_Jima

p. 146, Iwo Jima Map, Source: Sagredo 06:09, 31 December 2007 Source accessed December 31, 2018, https://commons.wikimedia.org/wiki/File:Iwo_jima_location_mapSagredo.png.

p. 148, Iwo Jima Landing Plan, Source: Center for the Public Domain. Accessed: December 31, 2018, https://commons.wikimedia.org/wiki/File:Iwo_Jima_-_Landing_Plan.jpg

p. 149, Bos, Carole. "To the Shores of Iwo Jima" AwesomeStories. com. Oct. 07, 2013. Accessed Jan 26, 2019, http://www.awesomestories. com/asset/view/To-the-Shores-of-Iwo-Jima.

p. 150, Photo 26-G-4140, U.S. Department of Transportation, U.S. Coast Guard, Office of Public and International Affairs. Accessed: December 31, 2018, https://en.wikipedia.org/wiki/Battle_of_Iwo_Jima

p. 152, Dempsey, David. *Time* magazine, April 1945 issue: cover story. Accessed January 25, 2019, http://time.com/3638523/ behind-the-picture-marines-blow-up-a-blockhouse-iwo-jima-1945/

p. 152, Nimitz, Chester. *Life* magazine, April 9, 1945 issue. Accessed January 25, 2019, https://dod.defense.gov/Photos/Photo-Gallery/ igphoto/2001157103/

p. 163, Longfellow, Henry Wadsworth. "The Village Blacksmith," accessed December 31, 2018, public-domain-poetry.com.

CPSIA information can be obtained
at www.ICGtesting.com
Printed in the USA
FSHW012020230319

9 781892 168238